A KID'S GUIDE TO

Storey Publishing

The mission of Storey Publishing is to serve our customers by publishing practical information that encourages personal independence in harmony with the environment.

Edited by Deanna F. Cook and Lisa H. Hiley
Art direction and book design by Alethea Morrison
Text production by Liseann Karandisecky
Indexed by Nancy D. Wood

Cover photography by © adogslifephoto/stock
    .adobe.com, spine; © damedeeso/iStock.com,
    back; © GlobalP/iStock.com, front; © poofy/
    stock.adobe.com, plaid pattern
Interior photography by Mars Vilaubi
Additional photography credits on page 144
Craft and food styling by Liseann Karandisecky
Cover and interior illustrations by © Ryan
    Wheatcroft, except, 44, 109, 110 by Ilona Sherratt

Storey books are available at special discounts when purchased in bulk for premiums and sales promotions as well as for fund-raising or educational use. Special editions or book excerpts can also be created to specification. For details, please call 800-827-8673, or send an email to sales@storey.com.

Storey Publishing
210 MASS MoCA Way
North Adams, MA 01247
storey.com

Printed in China through World Print
10 9 8 7 6 5 4 3 2 1

Library of Congress Cataloging-in-Publication Data

Names: Moore, Arden, author.
Title: A kid's guide to dogs : how to train, care for,
    and play and communicate with your amazing
    pet! / Arden Moore.
Description: North Adams : Storey Publishing,
    2020. | Includes index. | Audience: Ages 8–12 |
    Audience: Grades 4–6 | Summary: "This lively
    dog care book is packed with photos and colorful
    illustrations that teach training, care, health and
    safety, along with hands-on activities promoting
    play and bonding with canine companions"—
    Provided by publisher.
Identifiers: LCCN 2019032545 (print) | LCCN
    2019032546 (ebook) | ISBN 9781635860986
    (paperback) | ISBN 9781635860993 (hardcover) |
    ISBN 9781635861006 (ebook)
Subjects: LCSH: Dogs—Juvenile literature. | Dogs—
    Training—Juvenile literature.
Classification: LCC SF427 .M737 2020 (print) | LCC
    SF427 (ebook) | DDC 636.7/0835—dc23
LC record available at https://lccn.loc
    .gov/2019032545
LC ebook record available at https://lccn.loc
    .gov/2019032546

**I UNLEASH HEARTFELT
"PAWS AND APPLAUSE"**
to all the dogs in my life, past
and present, who have made
me a better person. Special
appreciation goes to my canine
writing partner for this book,
Kona, my sweet and smart Jack
Russell terrier mix.

And a big shout-out to my
pet-loving family, especially Julie,
Deb, Karen, Kevin, Jill, and Rick.

Contents

Hi, kids!

Arden and Kona

If you're reading this book, I bet you've always loved animals, just like me! One of my favorite memories is of the day my dad came home with a beagle he adopted from the local animal shelter. We named her Crackers. I'm not sure why we picked that name, but Crackers quickly became my best buddy.

She loved to join me on walks in the woods and swims in the lake. And she willingly helped me eat my beef liver (yuck!) without my parents noticing at dinner. Crackers was my first dog, and I will never forget her.

Today, I am blessed to share my life with three great dogs: Kona, Bujeau, and Cleo. Each day, they make me smile and teach me something new. For the past two decades, I have done my doggone best to educate people about dogs in my roles as a

pet behavior consultant, pet first-aid instructor, radio show host, and author. I believe I have the best job in the world!

Serving with me as your canine guide throughout this book is Kona, a happy, young Jack Russell terrier mix I adopted from an animal shelter in San Diego. It was love at first sight for me — and for her, first sniff.

At the time, Kona knew only one behavior cue — *Sit*. But since coming to live with me, Kona has mastered dozens of cues and tricks. She loves to learn! She has aced three levels of dog obedience training and delights in her role as a certified therapy dog when we visit schools, hospitals, and senior centers.

Her official title is Pet Safety Dog Kona, but she sports the fun nickname of "Ice Cream Kona." She travels with me all over the country as we teach pet first-aid classes and give pet behavior talks.

This shelter alum shines as a canine ambassador.

All dogs need and deserve a solid foundation of good training as well as opportunities to explore and play with their favorite person — you! Kona and I are here to give you the insights and tools you need to become your dog's best friend, whether you just brought home a new puppy or you've had a dog in the family for a long time, or even if you just love dogs and hope to have one of your own someday. Let the learning and fun activities begin!

Paws up!

Speak, Kona, Speak!

Hey, kids! We all know Arden couldn't have written this book without me. Look for my tips and comments throughout the book — I have plenty to say and am always happy to say it!

MY DOG, MY FRIEND

Sharing your life with a dog is totally cool. A dog can be your best friend — someone to love you, play with you, keep you company, and cuddle with when you're feeling sad. Many people consider their pets to be members of the family. I know I do.

Dogs score so many points when it comes to making our lives better. They are grrr-eat listeners who always seem to know how we're feeling. They can be four-legged comedians unleashing goofy antics. Even if your dog chews your favorite sweater or wakes you up early for a potty break, he will always view you as number one and treat you like the top dog.

Having a dog is more than just feeding and walking her and having cuddle time. It's important to understand her behavior and know how to treat her like a dog, not a furry person or a toy that you can pick up and play with whenever you want. Your dog, just like you, has feelings. She can feel happy and sad, confident and scared.

Because your dog — like all dogs — wasn't born with good manners or proper training, she counts on you and your family to teach her good canine habits. An important gift you can give your dog is positive, supportive training. With good training, you can keep your dog safer and make life easier and far more fun for the whole family — especially your dog! You'll learn about training in chapter 3. For now, let's talk some more about dogs.

LET YOUR DOG BE A DOG

You can have a great relationship with your dog, but it's different from the way you pal around with friends and the way you act with your siblings. Dogs are very attuned to humans. After all, they've been living with us for thousands of years! Even though they've adapted to living with us in close quarters, they have deep-seated needs that we must respect. Here are things to keep in mind about having a dog in your pack.

FAMILY RANKS

Keep in mind that dogs are pack animals who want and need to know their place in the family. Just like you know that your parents are the leaders of your family, your dog should know that your parents and you always "outrank" her. Playing the roles of benevolent leader and keeper of all treats is the way to earn canine respect and loyalty.

Your dog should never view herself as top dog in your household. That kind of canine confusion can cause problems. A dog who is confused or scared by not knowing how she fits into the family might become a dog who barks a lot, doesn't listen to anyone, chews up your stuff, runs away from you, or snaps at or even bites people. No one wants that! Dogs want and deserve family structure plus predictable daily routines.

A family is like a wolf pack — everyone needs to know where they stand in the group.

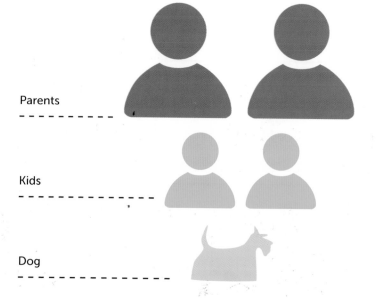

Parents

Kids

Dog

DOG SPEAK

What you say to your dog is not as crucial as *how* you say it. Dogs are highly attuned to emotions in people. Yelling at a dog is likely to cause her to cower submissively and tremble. Praising a dog will make her wag her tail with delight.

Dogs are also better at reading human body language and postures than people are at interpreting canine body language. So choose your words, tone, and body language carefully when "chatting" with your dog.

THINK LIKE A DOG

Dogs do their best to understand and interpret our behaviors. For example, to humans, hugging is a show of affection. But to a dog, a hug can be viewed as a threatening act, even if she puts up with it. For her, a good scratch on the chest or gentle petting on her back is more welcome. To help your dog on the path to becoming well behaved, it is important to respect her needs and to leave her alone when she wants to chill out or when she is eating.

Speak, Kona, Speak!

Dogs and people have been friends for a really long time! No one knows for sure, but most scientists think that humans had dogs as hunting partners and guardians as long as 14,000 years ago. Bow-WOW! That's a long time to be buddies!

Respect your dog. This terrier clearly doesn't want to be kissed. (Learn about body language on page 20.)

TRAINING = MORE FUN WITH FIDO!

Just as you learned from your parents to be polite and not interrupt people or shout indoors or run into the street, your dog needs help learning basic manners, too. Think about the benefits for you both. The better behaved you are, the more willing your parents are to take you places or let you take part in fun activities. The same goes for your dog. A well-trained, socialized dog is welcomed at many places, including dog-friendly hotels and restaurants, campgrounds, pet stores, beaches, and around town.

It's best if training starts in puppyhood, but it's never too late to teach an old dog new tricks!

MEETING AND GREETING DOGS

You may know your alphabet forward and backward, but do you know the doggy ABCs? As a dog-loving kid, you naturally want to say hello to any dog you see on the street, but you also need to keep safe and make sure the dog wants to say hello to you!

FOLLOW THESE THREE RULES to the letter every time you meet a dog to keep yourself safe and make the meet-and-greet fun for all. (For dog-to-dog meetings, see page 93.)

Let's say a cute dog on a leash is heading your way. Here's what to remember.

A = ASK PERMISSION. Never pet a dog you don't know unless the owner says it's okay to do so.

B = BE SNIFFED. Dogs use their strong sense of smell to determine if the person they are meeting is a friend or foe. Instead of immediately trying to pat the dog, make a fist and extend your hand for the dog to step forward to sniff.

C = CAREFULLY STROKE THE DOG'S BACK. Not all dogs like being patted on the head; it can feel threatening if they don't know you. Build up the dog's trust in you by gliding your hand gently down his back.

DO NOT PET THIS DOG

Some dogs do not want you to pet them. They may be afraid of strangers or just not interested in making friends. Keep on walking if a dog you meet shows these back-off signals:

* Hides behind his owner when you approach.
* Lunges or growls.
* Tenses his body.
* Raises his lip and shows his teeth.

BE A TREE

If a strange dog approaches you off leash, do not scream or run away. These actions will only cause some dogs to chase and possibly attack you. That's because dogs are predators, and they like to chase and capture prey that moves. So don't be prey! Stay still and be quiet.

Here's some good advice from our friends at Doggone Safe: Be a tree. Why act like a tree? A tree is boring because it just stands there. Dogs don't chase trees. They chase things that move, like squirrels. So even if you are scared when a strange dog approaches you, do your best to "be a tree" by following these three safety steps:

1. Stop and stay tall in place.
2. Slowly fold in your arms against your body.
3. Keep your head down and don't look directly at the dog.

WHAT THE YAP?

Dogs make about 15 different sounds, many of which they direct only at people. Why? Because dogs are smart. They have figured out that people communicate mostly by speaking rather than interpreting body postures. Dog-to-dog "conversations" tend to be silent because dogs mostly communicate with body postures.

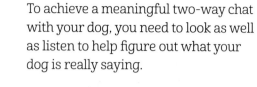

To achieve a meaningful two-way chat with your dog, you need to look as well as listen to help figure out what your dog is really saying.

ONE OR TWO BARKS. When your dog looks at you and barks just once or twice, she is trying to convey, "Hey, friend, what's up?" This is a doggy hello. Respond by greeting your dog in a friendly upbeat way to let her know you are paying attention. Keep it simple. Just say hi and your dog's name and give her a friendly pat.

A STRING OF RAPID BARKS. When your dog unleashes a bunch of bark-bark-barks that seem to speed up and go higher in pitch, she may be sounding the alert that a person or another dog is approaching. She could also be barking in frustration that her favorite tennis ball slid under the couch and she needs your help to retrieve it.

Resist trying to quiet her by yelling at her when she's in rapid-fire bark mode. In the dog world, yelling sounds like barking, and your dog is likely to interpret your excitement as an invitation to keep going.

WHINING. This high-pitched, mournful sound is made with a closed mouth. Doggy whines can be real calls for help, like when your dog is asking you to open the door so she can go out to potty. Sometimes dogs whine in frustration or because they are anxious about something, like waiting at the vet's office or being left outside a store when you go inside. Finally, dogs may whine when they are in pain, so check to see if your dog has an injury or a tender spot on her body.

PANTING. Dogs don't sweat through their skin the way people do. To cool off, they pant by breathing rapidly with an open mouth. A dog who is too hot or has been playing hard may pant quite heavily, a signal that it's time to rest and cool down and have some water.

Dogs may also pant when they are anxious or scared. Yawning or licking lips is another clue to nervousness.

HOWLING. Like their coyote and wolf ancestors, some dogs will raise their heads and let loose with a series of long-held notes. Some breeds, like Siberian huskies and beagles, are natural-born howlers. It's like a canine telephone system to communicate with faraway pack members.

Some breeds are natural-born howlers.

Dogs have much better hearing than humans, so some dogs howl when loud, high-pitched sounds like police sirens and fire truck horns irritate their sensitive ears. If your dog is a howler, you could train her to speak on cue and amaze your friends with her cool trick.

GROWLING. This low, rumbling sound comes from the throat, accompanied by lifted lips and bared teeth. It means "Stay away!" and is the warning a dog gives before she goes into attack mode. Do not approach a growling dog — she may lunge or even bite. Some dogs growl to guard food or their favorite possessions or to warn overly playful pups or children to leave them alone.

Speak, Kona, Speak!

My canine pals and I have plenty to yap about, but we often do it without making a sound. How? We do a lot of "talking" with body postures. And guess what? So do you! Think about waving to a friend to say hi, putting your finger to your lips to mean "shhhh," or jumping up and down with excitement (just like a happy dog!). Can you think of other examples of body language that dogs and people have in common?

Great Gravy Cookies

Your meat-loving dog will sit up and beg for this easy-to-make recipe.
Hey, where is it written that cookies must be sweet to taste good?

MAKES 4 DOZEN SMALL COOKIES

2½ cups whole-wheat flour, plus more for dusting

2 small jars beef-based baby food

6 tablespoons low-sodium beef gravy

½ cup nonfat dry milk

½ cup water

1 egg

1 tablespoon packed brown sugar

1 Preheat the oven to 350°F (180°C). Lightly coat a baking sheet with cooking spray.

2 Mix all the ingredients together in a large mixing bowl.

3 Dust your hands with flour and shape the dough into a big ball. Flatten the ball into a disc using a floured rolling pin.

4 Cut the dough into fun shapes with a cookie cutter.

5 Bake for 25 minutes, or until lightly browned. Allow the cookies to cool before serving.

Store in the refrigerator in an airtight container for up to two weeks. Serve one cookie a day for a dog up to 30 pounds; two cookies for a dog over 30 pounds. Break into small pieces to use for training treats.

19

DECODING BODY LANGUAGE

Wag more and talk less. That's what dogs do. Most of the time dogs "talk" silently by the way they move their heads, bodies, and tails. They usually save barking and other sounds for people. A notable exception is when a pack of friendly dogs at a dog park create a happy "barkfest" as they chase and play excitedly with one another.

But when it comes to conducting a clear conversation with your dog, you will need to figure out what he is saying by watching his whole body, from head to tail. This will give you a better idea of his mood and what he is trying to communicate. Look for this basic "vocabulary."

HEY, NICE TO SEE YOU! A welcoming dog wags his tail in a relaxed side-to-side direction or in a circle. His eyes are soft. He may greet you with a full-body wiggle or curve his body into a C shape. He may make singsong sounds or high quick barks or may lick your hand or cheek as a canine kiss.

WHAT'S UP? TELL ME MORE! Curious or interested dogs may tilt their heads when you talk as if to hear the words more clearly. They raise their tails up and wag them side to side. They often perk up their ears and relax their bodies. Some dogs will even lightly paw your arm or leg as if to show that they want to interact.

WANNA PLAY? Your dog plops into a play bow with his front legs stretched out on the ground and his rear end up in the air. His mouth is open and his tongue may be hanging out in what looks like a grin. He may push his nose against you or bring you his favorite toy or ball.

Some dogs will lift their heads and snap their jaws repeatedly — sounding like a crocodile! Look at the entire dog: often, you will see that in addition to this air snapping, the dog will make fun sideways dance moves and grab a toy and bring it to you to signal it's playtime.

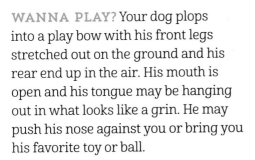

I'M NERVOUS OR ANXIOUS.

Scared or unsure dogs tuck their tails between their hind legs, lick their lips, yawn, and crouch down to appear smaller. They may also squint their eyes or avoid direct eye contact. They may pull their ears back.

Sometimes, they quiver or shake or may be so nervous that they can't control their bladder muscles and they pee a little. Some seem to freeze in place, while others will look desperately for a way to flee the scene. These are all ways of waving the white flag of surrender during an introduction.

Resist trying to comfort a scared dog by hugging or petting him or by using high-pitched baby talk — these actions can make him *more* nervous. Be calm, speak normally, and move slowly around this dog. Allow him to feel safe to approach you in his own time.

STAY AWAY FROM ME!

An angry or unfriendly dog may stare, display a tense body, push his ears forward or pin them back, raise his lips to show his teeth in a snarl, and/or hold his tail stiffly up in the air. He may lean forward on his front paws and even growl or bark loudly. These are all signals telling you to not approach.

TRIVIA
QUIZ 1

1. Who has more taste buds?

   A. People

   B. Dogs

   C. Cats

   D. They all have the same number of taste buds.

2. Which of these breeds can jump the highest?

   A. Jack Russell terrier

   B. German shepherd

   C. Golden retriever

   D. Greyhound

3. How many muscles does the average dog have in each ear?

   A. 4

   B. 8

   C. 12

   D. 16

4. Which of these dog breeds did not originate in the United States?

   A. Alaskan malamute

   B. Australian shepherd

   C. Basenji

   D. Rat terrier

See page 138 for answers.

A BIT ABOUT BREEDS

The *d* in *dog* could stand for "diversity"! Canines come in all shapes, sizes, hair types, and even personality tendencies. Look at the itty-bitty chihuahua and the looming Great Pyrenees. Then there's the curly-coated Portuguese water dog and the double-coated Siberian husky and that hairless breed with the hard-to-spell-and-say name: xoloitzcuintli (show-low-eats-QUEENT-lee)!

Speak, Kona, Speak!

Heed the breeds! We dogs come in lots of sizes, coat types, and even ear shapes. A breed is a type of dog that has been developed over many years to sport certain characteristics and traits, like a thick coat for warmth, or short, strong legs for digging out prey.

Here's a word to add to your doggy dictionary: Dogs with two parents of the same breed are called "purebred." What about me, you ask? Why, I'm a fan of plain old mutts, because I am one!

The American Kennel Club (AKC) recognizes nearly two hundred dog breeds, and the list of newly accepted breeds seems to grow each year. In addition to these recognized types, people have created a number of so-called designer breeds — a combination of two distinct breeds with the goal of creating a dog who exhibits the best of both breeds.

For example, mating a poodle with a schnauzer results in a litter of schnoodles. The offspring of a beagle and pug are known as puggles. And of course, there are always plain old mutts, who can be a combination of all kinds of different breeds. Their heritage is often a mystery, but they are usually terrific dogs.

When it comes to purebreds, the AKC recognizes seven distinct groups of dogs that have been bred to look a certain way and to exhibit certain personalities and skills.

Jack Russell and West Highland terriers

Cavalier King Charles spaniel

THE TERRIER GROUP

These dogs are known for their high energy, feistiness, and dogged determination. They were bred to hunt, kill vermin (sorry, trespassing rats), and guard their families. Examples are the cairn, West Highland white (a.k.a. Westies), Jack Russell, and Scottish terriers.

THE TOY GROUP

These dogs were bred to be cuddlers and lap loungers. Their small size makes them ideal for living in apartments and tiny houses and for traveling with their favorite people. But they can be big in personality. Popular examples include the Cavalier King Charles spaniel, the Chihuahua, and the Maltese.

THE WORKING GROUP

As the name implies, these dogs need a job to do. They often work as police dogs, search-and-rescue dogs, and bomb- or drug-sniffing dogs. This group includes such popular breeds as the Siberian husky, rottweiler, and boxer.

THE NON-SPORTING GROUP

This is the most diverse dog group with a variety of sizes, looks, and personalities. You really can't pinpoint one common trait in a group that includes such popular breeds as the schipperke, poodle, and bulldog.

Rottweiler

English bulldog

English springer spaniel

THE SPORTING GROUP

This group of dogs was bred to locate and retrieve real or pretend game of all sizes. Among the popular sporting breeds are the Labrador retriever, the golden retriever, and the English springer spaniel.

Poodle

THE HOUND GROUP

The common ancestral trait for dogs in this group is their ability to follow a trail and hunt. Most have a phenomenal sense of smell for tracking, while others rely more on their vision. The group includes the always-popular greyhound, bloodhound, dachshund, and beagle.

THE HERDING GROUP

These smart, energetic dogs were bred to control the movement of sheep, cattle, and other livestock on farms. They like to have a job to do and typically need a lot of exercise. Examples include the border collie, German shepherd, and two types of Welsh corgi.

Bloodhound

Border collies

FUN FACTS ABOUT 10 POPULAR BREEDS

Some dog breeds are more in demand than others. We shine a spotlight on 10 of the most popular.

BEAGLE. These small hunting dogs have an exceptional sense of smell and lots of energy. With their super noses, beagles can distinguish more than 50 different scents. Once they're on the scent, it can be hard to call them off, so they usually aren't reliable off leash, but at home they are friendly and playful.

Beagles were bred to have a white tip on their tails that makes it easier to see them running through high grass.

Beagle

BOXER. Sporting clownish faces and muscular bodies, boxers love activity. They get bored easily, so don't keep repeating the same trick with them. How did this breed get its name? These friendly dogs love to leap up and use their front paws to greet people. And their heads look a little like boxing gloves!

Most boxers love, love, love kids.

CHIHUAHUA. Ranked as the world's smallest breed, the Chihuahua averages two to six pounds. It originated in Mexico. Chihuahuas love to tunnel under blankets, pillows, and even dirty clothes in the hamper.

Chihuahua means "between two waters" in Spanish.

FRENCH BULLDOG. This cute, short-legged, round-bodied breed scores high in popularity and is known for its adorable "bat" ears as well as its pushed-in face and its snoring. This friendly dog loves to eat, but don't give in to those big eyes and ears and overfeed your pup.

Even though it's now known as the "Frenchie," its ancestor is the English bulldog.

GERMAN SHEPHERD. This herding breed loves to learn and work, which is why German shepherds make good police dogs. They are smart, strong, and loyal to their families. This breed sheds a lot, so step up your grooming skills by brushing your German shepherd at least twice a week.

The German shepherd is also known as the Alsatian.

GOLDEN RETRIEVER. One of the most popular breeds, golden retrievers are friendly, loyal, and intelligent. Originally bred for retrieving waterfowl, they are terrific swimmers. Golden retrievers lived in the White House with Presidents Gerald Ford and Ronald Reagan.

The world record for the loudest bark belongs to a golden named Charlie, whose bark was louder than a chain saw.

LABRADOR RETRIEVER. This very social breed loves kids and is often trained to be a service dog as well as a rescue dog to help find missing people. Most Labs love water and excel in dog sports like flyball, agility, and rally.

Labs come in three colors: yellow, chocolate, and black.

POODLE. The poodle is hailed as the national dog of France, but this breed originated in Germany as a hunting dog that retrieved game from water. Its name means "puddle" in German. Their soft coats shed very little, and they come in three sizes: toy, miniature, and standard.

Known for their smarts and athleticism, poodles learn tricks quickly and are often seen performing in dog acts.

YORKSHIRE TERRIER. Originating in Yorkshire, England, in the 1800s, the Yorkie is small in stature but big in bark. It was a tough little ratting dog before it became popular as a cuddly lap companion.

This breed has fine, silky hair that is grown quite long for the show ring.

JACK RUSSELL TERRIER. The Jack Russell is known for smarts, high energy, and quickness to bark. Officially called the Parson Russell terrier by the AKC, these independent thinkers like to be busy and can be a challenge to train. Jacks are usually white with brown or black patches and can have either a smooth or a rough coat.

Capable of leaping five feet in the air, this dog loves agility and other sports.

DiY
Dog Toys

Dogs love to play, and they deserve to have their own toys. They don't need tons of them, but they do like to have a few different ones to choose from (and chew on!). Try these easy-to-make homemade toys for your dog.

CRUNCH-MAKER TOY

Some dogs love a crinkly, crunchy toy! To make one, slip an empty plastic bottle inside a long sock or the cut-off sleeve of an old fleece or sweatshirt. Tie the open ends in big knots.

empty plastic bottle inside

TREAT PUZZLE TOY

1 Cut a few holes in a paper towel tube, making them just a little bigger than the treats.

2 Fold one end of the tube shut and put the treats inside.

3 Fold the other end shut and put the tube on the floor. How long does it take your dog to figure out how to release the treats by pawing at the toy?

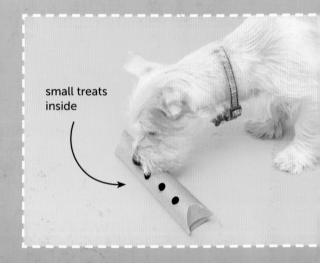

small treats inside

SOCK-IT-TO-ME TUG TOY

Tie a tight knot in the toe of a
long sock. Push a tennis ball
into the sock, down to the knot.
Tie another knot above the ball
and one at the open end of
the sock for a handle.
Let the tugging play
begin!

MAKE A HAPPY HOME
for Your Dog

It's important to know your dog's limits and to understand what it means to take care of her. Dogs crave routines. They may not wear watches, but they like to know when to expect breakfast and dinner, what time walks are, and where they are supposed to hang out when left home alone. Imagine how you would feel if you had to attend school at different times each day of the week or if your parents just forgot to make your dinner sometimes. Yikes, right?

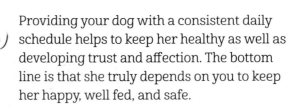

Providing your dog with a consistent daily schedule helps to keep her healthy as well as developing trust and affection. The bottom line is that she truly depends on you to keep her happy, well fed, and safe.

SIGN UP FOR DOG DUTY!

Living with a dog is a big responsibility. Your dog depends on you every day for food, water, exercise, and attention. You can't ignore him if you're feeling tired or lazy or even when you're sick. You need to be aware of what he needs and make sure he is happy and healthy.

If you are getting a new dog, work with your family to create a daily pet chore schedule before the arrival. If you already have a dog but no one is really in charge of taking care of him, it's not too late to take on the responsibility. Have everyone sign up for a job and post a weekly or monthly calendar where everyone can see it. Check off completed tasks each day, so you don't accidentally forget to do something. See the Chore Chart on the next page for an idea of what it takes to take care of a dog.

CHORE CHART

CHORE	MONDAY	TUESDAY	WEDNESDAY	THURSDAY	FRIDAY	SATURDAY	SUNDAY

Download and print the chore chart at www.storey.com/dog-chore-chart/.

POTTY TIME: When you wake up, usher your dog outside to go to the bathroom. Make this your first must-do.

CHOW TIME: Measure out his morning portion and ask him to sit politely before putting the bowl down.

WATER CHECK: Dump the old water, clean the bowl, and fill it up.

POOP PATROL: Arm yourself with a pooper scooper to pick up deposits every day.

WALKS: Aim for a 15- to 30-minute walk twice a day to give him time to do his business and enjoy the sights, sounds, and smells of the neighborhood.

TRAINING TIME: Schedule 10 to 15 minutes to reinforce a cue your dog knows like *Sit* or *Stay* or to introduce to a new cool trick, like *Belly up.*

CUDDLE AND PLAY TIME: Break out a toy for a romp in the yard or invite your dog to snuggle up as you watch a show or read a book.

GROOMING: Depending on your dog, you may need to comb or brush his coat daily, a few times a week, or weekly.

BATH TIME: Most dogs don't need regular baths, but if your dog gets extra dirty or rolls in something smelly, give him a bath with dog-safe shampoo.

Be a Super Pooper Scooper

Scooping poop is never a popular task, but doo-doo duties are very important. Most dogs poop two to three times a day, so it can really pile up. Left in the yard, poop can start to stink and attract flies — double yuck! Left along walkways or in the woods, it's a public nuisance and an environmental hazard.

If you love having a dog in the family, then it's only fair you do some of the dirty work. Scoop poop quickly by placing a small garbage can or five-gallon bucket lined with a plastic bag and a sturdy lid in a corner of the backyard. Do a daily poop patrol with a scooper and plop it into the can. Every week, tie up the whole bag and dispose of it in your main outdoor garbage.

Always pack extra poop bags on walks. It's easy to put one over your hand, pick up or scoop the pile, and turn the bag inside out, leaving the poop inside. Tie a knot and drop the bag in the trash. No big deal!

PET PROOFING 101

Dogs are as curious as, well, cats. They love to explore their surroundings using their powerful noses, keen eyes, and even their mouths. It takes just a second for a dog to chew up a shoe, raid a trash can, or dash out an open door. Work with your parents on pet proofing your house as well as your outdoor area. And patrol each room regularly to make sure there is nothing that can harm your canine friend.

KITCHEN

* Keep the trash under wraps in a covered container.
* Don't leave food unguarded on counters.
* Keep dogs out of the way when hot pots and pans are in use.

* Watch out for food snatching! See Ask the Vet, page 47, for a list of people foods that dogs shouldn't eat.
* A gate can keep your dog out of or in the kitchen as desired.

BATHROOM

* Keep the toilet lid down — it isn't a water bowl!
* Store cleaning materials and detergents out of reach.

I can explain.

LIVING AREA

* Tuck away exposed cords.
* Close fireplace doors or put up a screen so your dog can't get close to the flames.
* Position your dog's bed in a snug spot away from traffic.
* Put away chewable items like TV remotes and slippers.

BEDROOMS

* Stash your shoes and clothes where they belong. Many puppies and newly adopted dogs chew on their favorite person's belongings!
* Pick up small items like jewelry, hair clips, rubber bands, trading cards, small toys, and game pieces — anything that might tempt your dog.
* Charge your electronics out of reach, with the cords tucked away.

Speak, Kona, Speak!

Why do dogs chew up shoes, toys, and other favorite stuff of yours? When we're bored or have pent-up energy or feel anxious about being alone, it calms us down to chew on something that smells like someone we love. We know it makes you mad (and swallowing a sock can make us sick), but when stuff is lying around, we can't always help ourselves. But *you* can help us by putting dirty laundry in the hamper and picking up your toys. That'll make your parents happier, too!

And please give us a sturdy, dog-safe toy or bone to occupy our time while we wait for you to come home. On behalf of dogs (and shoes) everywhere, I thank you.

Unsafe Indoor Plants

These common plants aren't good for dogs to snack on. Make sure they are out of reach.

* Aloe
* Amaryllis
* Sago palm
* Philodendron and pothos
* Rubber tree
* Jade tree
* Dumb cane (*Dieffenbachia*)
* Asparagus fern
* Corn plant (*Dracaena*)
* Ivy

IS YOUR YARD CANINE READY?

If you have a backyard, you and your dog will spend a lot of time playing out there, so keep it safe.

PUT UP A GOOD FENCE. The most important thing is to have a good fenced-in area where your dog can play off leash. Even the sweetest, most loyal dog may turn into a Houdini hound and pull a disappearing act. Whenever your dog is in the yard, make sure the gate is securely latched.

INSPECT YOUR YARD OFTEN. Make sure your dog cannot dig under the fence or use a piece of lawn furniture as a launching pad to jump over the fence and escape. Store all mulch, fertilizers, and compost in areas your dog cannot get into.

PLANT DOG-SAFE PLANTS. Check out your yard to make sure there aren't any plants that are toxic to pets. For more information, visit the ASPCA Animal Poison Control Center (see Resources).

WATCH OUT FOR THESE PLANTS

If your family is outside doing some gardening, make sure plants are safe for your pets. You might be surprised to learn that these common plants can make your dog sick if he chooses to chomp on them.

Crocus, daffodil, and tulip — the whole plant, but especially the bulb

Azalea and rhododendron

Deadly nightshade

Oleander

Buttercup

Yew

Holly

Foxglove

DiY
Doggy Bed
Don't Retire That Tire

Store-bought doggy beds can be pricey and impersonal. Here and on the next page are do-it-yourself ideas using recycled materials to create a cozy, customized bed for your pal.

An old tire

Nontoxic paint

A thick pillow or large blanket

A pillowcase or large piece of fabric

1 Scrub the tire clean with soapy water. Rinse it and allow it to dry completely.

2 Paint it your favorite color and let the paint dry. (You may need two coats.)

3 Decorate it, maybe with your dog's name.

4 Stuff the pillow or blanket into the pillowcase or wrap it in the fabric. Adjust the pillow in the center of the tire to make a comfy bed.

DiY

Doggy Bed

Give New Life to an Old Suitcase

An old suitcase makes the perfect bed for snoozing at home or taking along on a road trip.

A hard-sided suitcase, large enough for your dog to turn around in

Things to decorate with (fabric or felt, elastic, glue or staples, sewing supplies)

A pillow that fits snugly

A pillowcase or piece of fabric

1 Decorate the interior lid of the suitcase. The one on the facing page has a simple pocket glued in place for holding toys.

2 Stuff the pillow into the larger side of the suitcase and smooth out the fabric.

3 To keep the lid from closing, attach a block of wood or a strap of fabric to the back of the suitcase with heavy-duty glue.

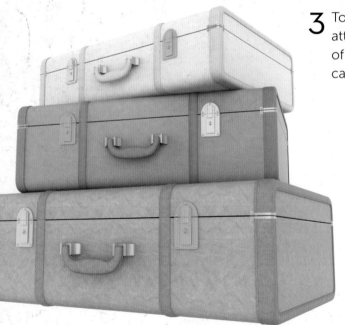

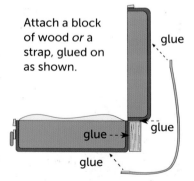

Attach a block of wood *or* a strap, glued on as shown.

glue

glue

glue

glue

MAKE YOUR DOG'S CRATE GRRR-EAT!

An unsupervised dog can get into mischief — like chewing your favorite T-shirt or raiding the garbage can. He needs a safe place to chill when he's alone in the house. They also need a place to go when it's time to "settle" (see page 74 for more about that). People don't like being confined, but most dogs appreciate a cozy, protected space. This is where a dog crate comes in.

A crate needs to be big enough for your dog to stand and turn around. Line the bottom with a cushy pad or blanket. To show him that the crate is a welcoming place, toss a treat or a chew toy inside. When he goes in, gently close the crate door and praise him. A few seconds later, open the door and let him come out. Gradually build up his time in his crate so he gets the idea that this is his very own wonderful canine condo.

When training your dog to stay in his crate, try feeding him it in, opening the door as soon as he's done eating. This provides two key benefits: you can keep an eye on your dog at mealtime, and it prevents other pets in the house from taking his food. Associating a positive experience — eating — with the crate makes it a welcoming space.

Never use the crate for punishment. Depending on the size of the crate, your dog can ride in it during road trips and happily hang out in the hotel room when your family heads out without him.

Speak, Kona, Speak!

You know how you don't like your sibling getting into your stuff? Well, you're kind of like your dog's two-legged brother or sister, and I have a big request. Please, please, please do not crawl into your dog's cozy crate or try to share his doggy bed. It may feel like a cool play fort to you, but just like you, we dogs need our own spaces. Our crate or bed is like our private bedroom where we feel safe enough to take a catnap. Yep, I said "catnap"!

ASK THE VET

I love giving my big dog, Dolly, lots of treats. How many treats are too many for her? I don't want her to have a tummy ache.

— Ryan, age 5, Dallas, Texas

That's a great question, because just like you, Dolly can get a stomachache from eating too many treats and can become overweight. Here's one way to give her treats: Measure out Dolly's dry food for the day. Give her half of it in the bowl, like you normally do, and give her the other half as treats during the day.

Frozen green beans or pieces of carrot are a healthy snack that many dogs enjoy. For some special treats you can make for your dog, check out the recipes on pages 19, 78, 112, 113, and 114.

But be careful: not all people food is safe for dogs. Keep Dolly away from sugary foods, caffeine, fatty meat, onions, grapes and raisins, dark chocolate, avocados, and macadamia nuts.

The best treat that you can give your dog is spending time with her and showing her lots of love.

— Dr. Liz Bales, Red Lion Veterinary Hospital, New Castle, Delaware

3

TIME FOR SCHOOL
The Canine ABCs

Dogs and kids have a lot in common, like loving to play and being happy to be with friends and family. And like kids, dogs need an education. You just attend different types of schools. In your dog's case, you are the teacher! Your dog depends on you to school him for success. While it's great if you can start from scratch with a new puppy, it's always possible to teach new behaviors to a dog, even one who has learned some bad habits.

Your dog needs and deserves to learn these basic canine commands: *No*, *Watch me*, *Off*, *Sit*, *Stay*, *Come*, *Walk nicely* (*Heel*), and *Settle*. With your help, your dog will soak up knowledge like a sponge and you can show off his new abilities to your pals!

WHY DO DOGS NEED GOOD MANNERS?

Learning how to behave keeps your dog safe and makes her more fun to be around. Think about it: How much trouble can your canine pal get into if she's sitting politely? Exactly! A sitting dog won't jump up on people when they come through your door or rush to greet a small child who may be afraid of her.

Your dog will be easier to care for if she sits politely for your *Okay* cue (see page 54) at mealtime. It's more fun getting ready for a walk if she plops down when you bring out the leash instead of going bananas and racing around the house. When you come home from a muddy walk, you'll appreciate a dog who sits patiently while you wipe her feet with a towel (or even flops over on her back — see Teaching *Belly Up*, page 86).

A dog who comes when you call is a safe dog: she won't dart into traffic and get injured or run up to a leashed dog and possibly start a fight. Plus, you'll both have more fun going on long walks if she can be off leash wherever it's allowed.

A well-behaved dog can enjoy fun outings, like visiting friends, playing at dog parks, and going to dog-friendly stores and restaurants. Begging at the table may seem cute, but it's a bad habit. A dog who knows how to settle quietly in her spot during dinner isn't putting her nose on the table looking for a handout.

You'll be proud when you hear people say, "What a good dog!" instead of "You need to teach that dog some manners!"

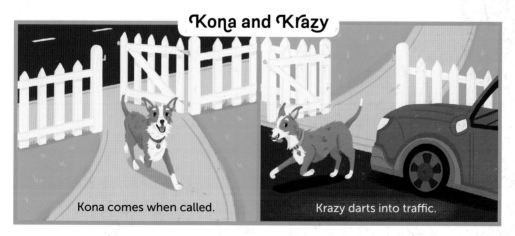

Kona and Krazy

Kona comes when called.

Krazy darts into traffic.

49

PRACTICE THE THREE Cs

When training, it's important to practice what I call the Three Cs: be concise, be consistent, and be clear. Predictability is a big deal for dogs. They are constantly reading our body postures and the tone of our voices to do their best to interpret what we are conveying. If you give mixed signals, your dog will be confused.

1. BE CONCISE. Dogs understand a lot of what we say, but they don't speak English! Pick one word for each behavior and stick with that cue. If you say "Chipper, please sit! Can you sit? Sit, girl! Sit, sit, sit! Hey, I told you to sit!" all Chipper hears is "Blah, blah, blah, blah!"

Chipper, please sit! Can you sit? I said, sit!

blah, blah, blah, blah

2. BE CONSISTENT. Training a behavior takes a lot of repetition. Your dog will understand what you want a lot sooner if you pair the same cue with the same action every time. For example, one way to teach *Sit* is to hold a treat in front of your dog's face and slowly raise the treat over your dog's head. He'll keep looking up until his butt hits the ground.

Immediately reward him by saying "Good sit!" and handing over his reward. Do the same thing every time his butt touches the ground. If you say, "Good sit!" too soon, such as when he first puts his head up to see the treat, he'll think that *Sit* means "Look at this treat." If he doesn't immediately sit, count to 10 in your head to give him some time to process your request. (See page 60 for more.)

3. BE CLEAR. Don't repeat the cue over and over if your dog doesn't do what you want right away. If your dog runs away from you and you start yelling "Come, come, come, come" while chasing after him, he's learning that *Come* means "I'm going to chase you — what a fun game!" In training, you often need to break down each behavior into smaller parts so that your dog knows what you want.

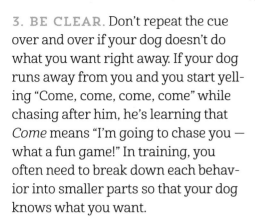

Speak, Kona, Speak!

Woof! Hello! Hola! Did you know dogs are multilingual? We speak Dog, of course, but we all know some human words, and some of us know even more. In fact, I speak five languages: Dog, English, Spanish, sign language, and a little Cat.

After Arden taught me *Sit* and *Come*, she started adding the Spanish words, *Sentado* and *Veni*, to those cues. Then she paired hand signals with those cues. Now when we're at a busy, noisy place or a very quiet one, Arden can communicate with me without saying a word. As for Cat, I know to approach my feline sibs when they're purring and to back off if they hiss!

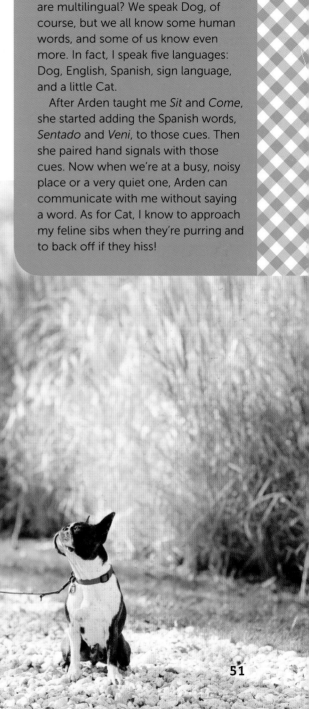

SIT!

"GOOD DOG!"

Here's a major tip to help your dog become an A student: reward your dog for good behavior instead of punishing her when she does something wrong. Dogs are born pleasers. They live for our approval. They are motivated to learn when the training is fun and when the trainer — you — is being friendly and patient.

Animal behaviorists have proven that dogs learn best with positive reinforcement. That means teaching behaviors you want with praise and treats, not yelling at them when they make mistakes. Dogs quickly learn that rewards occur when they do the right thing, which makes them want to work and figure out how to earn rewards.

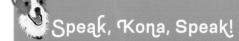

Speak, Kona, Speak!

In many ways, we dogs are a lot like kids. I bet you give your best effort when your teachers encourage you by saying, "Good job," "You can do it," or "Just take it one step at a time."

It's a lot easier to listen and more fun to learn when training sessions are short and full of praise. When you focus on reinforcing the good instead of pointing out the mistakes, your dog will be more inspired to learn new obedience cues and cool tricks.

Am I a good boy? Am I? Am I?

LET'S START CANINE ACADEMY

Start your lessons in a quiet spot in your home or yard where you both can concentrate. As your dog learns, find new places to train where there are more distractions — it's important that your dog knows how to behave in all kinds of situations.

Hold your training sessions when you aren't feeling rushed or impatient. Try for at least one session a day, but breaking training into several shorter lessons will be more fun and often less frustrating for both of you.

Keep the mood positive and have plenty of bite-sized healthy treats to reward your dog. Your dog will be more motivated if you hold training sessions before meals so she's a little bit hungry.

Be supportive by proclaiming **Good!** when your dog does what you ask her to do. Pair that word with the training cue, for example *Good sit!* Always use a happy, upbeat voice so your dog knows you're pleased with her.

Quit on a good note. That means ending each lesson after your dog has been successful, instead of being discouraged if you can't make her understand what you want. If you're having trouble, go back to a behavior she knows so you can praise her for doing it right. Dogs don't like being frustrated any more than you do!

TEACHING OKAY

Your dog needs to have some type of signal to indicate when class is over and he has permission to be goofy or play or go somewhere and relax. It's like a thumbs up or a head nod from a teacher or coach. For a dog, *Okay* (both spoken and as an open hand gesture) plays a pivotal role in training.

The *Okay* cue is a quick way to release a dog who is obediently holding a sit, stay, or down position. Your cue tells him that he can do something else, like go gobble up a treat dropped on the floor or play with a toy.

It is important for dogs to comprehend both hearing and seeing the *Okay* signal.

1 **The easiest gesture is to hold your hand palm up at chest level.**

Speak, Kona, Speak!

I'm A-OK with *Okay*. Arden taught me this cue when she first adopted me. When we're doing a pet behavior talk in a classroom, I know to hold a sit in the back of the room as Arden walks to the front of the room. Our eyes meet, but I know not to move until she says *Okay* or moves her open hand to the side. The kids love it when I dash past them to reach her!

2 **Then sweep it sideways while turning your thumb up.** Use the gesture consistently when you give the verbal cue and your dog will soon connect them.

TRIVIA
QUIZ 2

1. When a dog sniffs another dog's rear end, what is he "downloading" about the other dog?

A. His mood

B. What he ate for breakfast

C. Any health problems

D. All of the above

E. None of the above

2. Dogs can see in total darkness.

A. True

B. False

3. How many taste buds do dogs have?

A. 17

B. 170

C. 1,700

4. How many eggs can a female flea produce in just one day?

A. 15

B. 25

C. 50

D. 65

5. Dogs sometimes have sweaty feet.

A. True

B. False

See page 138 for answers.

TEACHING NO

In dog land, *No* is a must-learn word. It's a quick cue to let your dog know to stop what she's doing — now! This command puts the brakes on unwanted behavior like picking up something yucky on the sidewalk to eat. You'll need two kinds of treats, one that your dog thinks is okay, like kibble, and one that she'll really go for, like a slice of hot dog.

1 **Hold the okay treat in the open palm of your hand about six inches from your dog's mouth.**

2 **When she moves forward to take the treat, close your fist and firmly say *No*.**

Don't yell. If she attempts to mouth or paw at your hand, keep your fist closed and just wait.

Be patient. Most dogs give up after about 10 seconds.

3 Open your hand to show her the treat again, quickly closing your hand into a fist if she moves toward the treat.

Do this several times. Give your dog time to figure out what is happening and how she should respond. Some dogs learn quicker than others.

4 Once your dog stops going after the treat in your hand, reward her with a couple of the better treats from the pouch, marking the action with the word *Okay*.

TEACHING WATCH ME

Before you can teach a dog anything, you have to have her attention. *Watch me* is an often-overlooked training cue, but if your dog knows this cue, it will help your training. Whenever you want to get your dog's attention to start a new training session, begin with *Watch me*. This cue also helps your dog improve his focus on you and not on distractions in your home or in the environment when you are both out and about.

1 **Hold a treat in your hand to get your dog's attention.**

You may need to wave it in front of his nose, but most dogs will be watching you already, perhaps drooling a little in anticipation.

2 **Keeping your eyes on your dog's face, slowly bring the treat near your eye as you say *Watch me.***

3 As soon as your dog locks eyes with you, quickly say *Good watch me!* and hand over the treat.

After he has aced this a few times in a row, make him wait a couple of seconds before rewarding him.

Did I hear "food"...I mean "Watch me"?

Speak, Kona, Speak!

This is a fun one! Whenever Arden says, "Kona, *Watch me*," I quickly lock eyes with her, knowing I'll score a yummy payoff. Here are some inside tips:

✳ If your dog looks away before you give him the treat, show it to him again and repeat the steps.

✳ Always make sure he is looking at you when you give him the treat so he understands what you want.

✳ Don't overdo it. Practice a few times, then move on to the next thing.

TEACHING SIT

When a dog is sitting, she can't get into trouble. She is in the parked position. This is one of the most important cues to teach your dog. Resist trying to push down her rump — your dog may think you're trying to play, or she may feel nervous and try to get away. (See page 65 for reasons to teach *Sit*.)

1 **Position your dog so she's facing you.**

2 **Hold a treat in front of your dog's nose.**

3 **Say *Sit* as you slowly lift the treat above her head.** Let gravity do its job. As your dog moves her head up to follow the treat, her rump will sink to the floor.

4 **As soon as she sits,** immediately mark the action by saying *Good sit!* and handing over the treat.

Once your dog is sitting promptly at your cue, start making her wait a few seconds before rewarding her.

TEACHING **DOWN**

Once your dog is happily heeding your requests to "park it," you are ready to teach him the very important *Down* cue. Dogs who lie down when asked are welcome in pet-friendly places because they don't get into any mischief. Here's a tip: Some dogs don't like putting their bellies on a hard surface. Encourage your dog by holding your training sessions in a carpeted room or on a large towel or blanket.

1 **Ask your dog to sit facing you.** Bring a treat close to his face. Say *Down* and slowly move the treat straight to the floor. As his nose follows the treat, he may lie down to reach it.

Move treat down, then away in an L-shape.

2 **If he does plop down on his own, quickly say** *Good down!* and hand over the treat while he is still lying down. If he stands up, ask him to sit and start again.

Nope! Let's try again!

3 If he doesn't lie down immediately, calmly hold the treat on the floor to give him time to figure out that he needs to lie down to reach it.

Heap on the praise as soon as he does — and hand over the treat, of course! Repeat these steps several times in a few short training sessions until your dog is consistently moving from a sit to a down.

Almost!

4 Now you can start adding duration and distance. Delay for a few seconds each time your dog goes into a down before handing over the treat.

And then practice taking a step or two away before you say *Down* while you move your hand holding the treat toward the floor.

Good boy!

TEACHING OFF

You might think it's cute when a puppy or a tiny dog jumps up to greet you, but it's less fun when the dog is big or muddy. Your guests will appreciate being greeted politely by your dog without being knocked over. Instead of yelling at him, the trick is to teach your dog to do something else, like sit. You'll need a long leash (at least six feet) and a helper.

1 **Attach the leash to your dog's collar or harness.** Stand behind your dog holding the leash in your hand.

Have your helper approach your dog from the front, without bending over or trying to pet him.

It's good to practice this with different helpers.

2 **As soon as your dog starts to jump up toward the person, say** *Off!* and quickly pull the leash straight down and to the side. The goal is to stop your dog from moving forward and up.

Reasons to Teach Your Dog to "Park It"

S-i-t. This three-letter word is key to keeping your new pup or dog safe and well-mannered. After all, how can your canine pal get into mischief when he is sitting? Teaching your dog to hit the park position on your command yields many benefits. With proper training, your dog will be good at:

✳ Greeting guests politely at the door instead of jumping up on them.

✳ Showing good mealtime manners by waiting for his dish to be put down.

✳ Staying safely put when the car door is open so you can put on his leash before escorting him out.

✳ Sitting politely when you bring out the leash for a walk instead of going bananas and racing around the house.

✳ Holding still so you can clean his muddy paws before coming in the house. (Your parents will really like this reason!)

✳ Garnering praise out in public for being such a well-behaved dog!

Whatever you say, Boss!

3 **The second your dog has all four paws on the floor, tell him to *Sit* and reward him right away when he does.**

In time, your dog will learn that he scores no attention from visitors and no treats when he leaps up, but he is rewarded with pats and treats when he sits politely to greet people.

TEACHING STAY

The goal of this cue is to keep your dog from taking another step. This is important when you want your dog to wait patiently while you do something else. It is challenging to teach, but be patient. Start with your dog on a leash and ask for just a few seconds of holding the position, then gradually increase the amount of time. After your dog learns to stay while leashed, practice for a while without holding on to the leash, then move on to practicing with no leash.

1 Leash your dog, place her at your side, and say *Sit*.

2 Toss a treat or two just out of her reach in front of her. Say *Stay*.

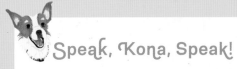

3 **If she pulls toward the treat, don't say anything.** Calmly hold on to the leash so that she can't move forward. Wait until she stops pulling and stays seated in place.

4 **Once she holds her position for just a few seconds,** say *Good stay* and then *Okay* as you loosen the leash so she can get the treat.

(CONTINUED)

67

5 **When she will stay while eyeing a treat in front of her,** keep hold of the leash as you say *Stay* and toss a treat about two feet in front of her.

6 **When she stops trying to reach the treat,** say *Good stay*, then *Okay* as you loosen the leash so she can retrieve her reward. When she has learned to sit and stay, practice *Stay* from the down position.

ASK THE VET

Why do dogs pant?

— Sadie, age 7, Chicago, Illinois

Have you ever seen a sweaty dog? I bet not! That's because dogs don't sweat like people do. While dogs may sweat a little bit from their paws, it's not enough to cool them off when the weather gets hot. Dogs cool themselves down by breathing in cooler air and panting to release warmer air from their bodies.

Believe it or not, panting is also a way for a dog to communicate. Even if the weather is cool, dogs may pant to tell other dogs that they are feeling nervous. Dogs also pant when they are very excited or if they are really happy.

If a dog is panting too much, it may be because he isn't feeling well. But most of the time dogs pant just to keep themselves cool.

— Dr. Lisa Lippman, house call veterinarian, New York, New York

TEACHING COME

Coming when called is a crucial lesson if your dog enjoys playing off leash. A dog who runs all over the place ignoring you is a dog who can easily get into trouble or be injured. In obedience terms, a dog who "has a good recall" is one that comes on command.

It's important to train this cue in stages, starting in a quiet, confined area and slowly moving to larger spaces with more distractions. Start your sessions with a 12- to 20-foot leash or clothesline that can be safely tethered to your dog's collar or harness. Work on refining your recall off leash in a confined area until you are very confident that your dog will return when called.

Speak, Kona, Speak!

Come can be a tough command, especially for a dog who is easily distracted by interesting sights and smells — and that's pretty much all of us! My advice is to practice, practice, practice, and keep these tips in mind:

* A good way to reinforce the cue is to call your dog, reward her, and then let her go have some more fun.

* Always make it worthwhile for your dog to come back to you, even if you just pile on the praise.

* Even if she's been running away or ignoring you, praise her when she does come to you. If you yell at her then, she'll think she's in trouble for coming, not for the other stuff.

1 **Cue your dog to *Sit* and *Stay* while facing you.** Slowly walk backward about five feet from him as you hold on to the leash.

70

2 In an enthusiastic tone, say your dog's name and *Come!* Bend forward to encourage him, but don't repeat the command.

3 When he reaches you, say *Good come!* and hand him a treat. Practice in short sessions until he understands that *Come* means to head right to you.

4 Once he'll come consistently from a stay position, practice calling him from farther away.

The next step is to let him wander away from you, still on the leash, before you call him. If he isn't paying attention, you can give a gentle tug on the leash as you call him.

Eventually you can drop the leash while he drags it (so you can grab it if you need to) and then progress to practicing off leash.

TEACHING WALK NICELY (HEEL)

You don't want your dog yanking on the leash or refusing to budge. You are walking your dog — not the other way around! *Heel* is an old-fashioned term that hunters used to keep their hunting dogs close by their sides. A more polite and modern way to describe a dog walking next to you on a loose leash is *Walk nicely*.

Start training this behavior in a familiar spot with few distractions, like your yard or the sidewalk near your house. Once your dog is walking nicely close to your house, try walking her down other streets during a quiet time of day. Eventually you can practice in more distracting settings.

1 **Start by letting your dog walk on a loose leash.** If she starts to pull, stop walking and wait for her to look back at you. Say *Good watch me* and hand her a small treat.

Your goal is to reinforce that it's more important to pay attention to you than to distractions like a squirrel.

2 **The next step is to add the phrase *Walk nicely* as you first step off.** As you walk, hold a treat just in front of her nose to keep her close by your side.

Clicker Training Is Cool!

A fun way to teach your dog basic cues and cool tricks is clicker training. A clicker is a metal device you hold in your hand that makes a distinctive sound when you press it. The first step is teaching your dog that the clicker sound means a tasty treat is coming. Most dogs learn that pretty quickly!

The next step is pressing the clicker whenever your dog does something you want him to do, such as wave his paw or stay on a mat. The clicking sound "marks the behavior" and lets your dog know that he's done something right and will get a reward.

The beauty of clicker training is that you can use it to shape behavior and train very specific tricks. And it gets you into the habit of paying attention to what your dog is doing so that you can reward him. If you don't have a clicker, no worries. You can make a clucking sound with your tongue against the roof of your mouth or click a ballpoint pen.

The key to clicker training is timing. You need to dole out the treat as soon as your dog does the desired action. But don't worry — in obedience classes, kids often get the hang of the clicker faster than adults!

3 **After she walks next to you — not ahead of you — for a few steps, say *Good walk nicely* and hand her the treat.**

Slowly increase the number of steps between rewards.

If she starts to pull, just stop and wait for her to realize that you're not going anywhere unless she's walking next to you.

TEACHING SETTLE

This cue tells your dog it's time to head for her bed or blanket, lie down, and chill. When we're traveling and teaching class, Kona knows that *Settle* means she can relax and be off duty for a while. This behavior combines *Down* and *Stay*, so make sure your dog knows those commands before starting to train this one.

1 **Practice near your dog's bed or a favorite blanket folded on the floor.**

Stand two or three feet from the bed with your dog sitting beside you. Toss a treat onto the bed. Say *Settle* as you point to the bed to encourage your dog to go toward it.

2 **Let her eat the treat, then say *Down* to cue her to lie on the bed.** After a few seconds, say *Good settle!* as you give her another treat to reinforce the desired action.

3 **Practice until your dog associates the tossed treat with your pointing toward the bed.** Then stop tossing the treat as you point and wait to reward her for going over and lying down.

Once she is doing that consistently, you can tell her to *Stay* once she lies down. Gradually extend the amount of time you expect her to stay on the bed before you reward her.

4 **You are now ready to expand this cue** by pointing to a different spot where you would like her to lie down and stay.

Repeat the above steps to reinforce that your pointing hand paired with the word *Settle* indicates where she should lie down.

SIGN UP FOR OBEDIENCE CLASS

A great way to strengthen your bond with your dog is to enroll in an obedience class led by a professional trainer who uses positive reinforcement. These classes expose you and your dog to new dogs, people, and locations — all pluses in helping your dog become well socialized. The trainer will give you individualized, step-by-step instruction for teaching your dog the must-know canine commands.

Expect some homework with these classes. But this is fun homework that you get to do with your dog after school and on weekends. With the following tips in mind, you and your dog are sure to succeed:

ARRIVE EARLY so your dog can sniff the grounds and go potty before starting class.

BRING A TREAT POUCH. Fill it with bite-sized treats and fasten it around your waist for quick access.

BE IN THE MOMENT. Don't fret if your dog misses a cue or is distracted by another dog. Listen to the trainer and focus on the *now*.

RESPECT THE BOUNDARIES of other canine students. Just like people, dogs sport a wide range of personalities. Some are friendly, some are shy, some are bossy, and some are easily excitable. Ask if it's okay to pet another dog or let your dog try to make friends.

HANG UP ON SOCIAL MEDIA. Post updates on Facebook, Twitter, Instagram, and other outlets *after* class is over. Your dog (and the instructor) needs you to be paying attention.

Is Your Dog a Canine Genius?

Have you got a four-legged Einstein? Or is your canine pal a happy average student? Of course, you love your dog no matter what his IQ, but here is a fun way to test canine intelligence. You need a 12-cup muffin pan, a handful of treats, and 12 tennis balls.

1. Have your dog sit with the muffin pan in front of him.

2. Let him watch you place a treat in six or seven of the muffin cups.

3. Cover each of the cups with a tennis ball to hide the treats.

4. Tell your dog *Okay, find the treats*! Time how long it takes him to nose off the tennis balls from the holes containing treats.

Munchy Pup-Cakes

This dog-friendly version of carrot cake probably isn't sweet enough for most kids, but dogs gobble them up, with or without frosting.

MAKES 12 MUFFINS

½ **cup water**

1 **large carrot, shredded**

1 **egg**

½ **teaspoon vanilla extract**

1 **tablespoon honey**

1 **large ripe banana, mashed**

2 **cups whole-wheat flour**

½ **teaspoon baking powder**

½ **teaspoon ground nutmeg**

½ **teaspoon ground cinnamon**

1 Preheat the oven to 350°F (180°C). Spray a 12-cup muffin pan with cooking spray.

2 Blend the water, carrot, egg, vanilla, and honey in a large mixing bowl. Stir in the banana.

3 Mix the flour, baking powder, nutmeg, and cinnamon together in a separate bowl.

4 Pour the flour mixture into the carrot mixture and mix thoroughly.

5 Fill each cup of the prepared pan about three-quarters full. Bake for 50 to 60 minutes, or until a toothpick inserted in the center of a cupcake comes out clean.

6 Remove from pan and let cool before serving. For an extra-special treat, frost them with the Bow Wow Brownie Frosting on page 113.

Serving size is ½ cupcake for dogs under 30 pounds; 1 cupcake for dogs above 30 pounds.

TRICKS FOR TREATS!

Once your canine pal has aced the basic obedience cues, you can start working on all kinds of cool new tricks. The more she knows, the more she'll want to learn! The sky's the limit on what you can teach her. Invest a few minutes each day focusing on one trick at a time to help your dog expand her number of tricks.

On the next few pages, you'll find step-by-step guides for teaching your dog some "bone-a-fide" crowd-pleasing tricks.

Speak, Kona, Speak!

Here's a little insight into a dog's life: We live in the present tense. We don't spend time thinking about the past, and we certainly aren't thinking about the future. We dogs are also "paw-some" at forgiving and forgetting — and we do our best to help you live in the moment, especially when you are hanging out with us!

Charmed to meet you, darling.

TEACHING SHAKE

Here is a fun way to teach your dog to say hello to your friends. It starts with the basic canine handshake and then adds a crowd-pleasing wave. Start by mastering the canine handshake.

1 **Have your dog sit facing you.** Kneel down and lift his right front paw into the air with your left hand. As you pick up his paw, say *Shake* and give him a treat. Do this a few times.

2 **Next, take a treat in your left hand.** Without touching him, move your hand slowly toward his right front paw. Stop and wait for him to lift his paw off the ground.(If he only sniffs at the treat, wait patiently for him to realize that you want him to raise his paw.)

3 **Quickly take his paw in your right hand and say *Good shake* as you hand over the treat.** If necessary, go back to step 1. Treat and praise your dog each time he lifts his paw off the floor for you to take.

TEACHING WAVE

Once your dog is consistently lifting his paw, you can add some adorable paw motion.

1 Instead of taking his paw, say *Wave* and slowly move the treat from side to side to encourage your dog to touch the treat with his paw.

2 If he moves his raised paw even a little, say *Good wave* and hand him the treat. Keep praising and treating as he gets the idea that you want him to move his paw back and forth.

3 After a while, you can reward him after several waves. Don't expect him to do more than a few at a time, though.

TEACHING
WEAVE THROUGH YOUR LEGS

If your dog acts like your shadow and always seems to want to be close by your side, she may be a good candidate to learn the art of weaving in and out of your legs. Your goal is to have your dog perform a figure eight through your legs. As with all training, it starts with one step at a time!

1 **Cue your dog to *Sit* facing you up close.** Stand tall with your legs wide apart.

2 **Holding a treat in your left hand, tuck your hand behind your left leg, so your dog can see the treat.**

Say *Weave* as you encourage her to reach through your legs for the treat.

3 When she pokes her head through your legs, say *Good weave* and reward her. At first just work on having your dog follow the treat through your legs. Always make it playful and fun.

4 Once your dog knows to follow your hand, position her so she is sitting on your right side and looking up at you. Hold a treat in your left hand.

5 Take a big step forward with your left leg and lower your left hand under your outstretched leg to entice your dog to put her head through your legs. If she doesn't understand what you want at first, hold the treat closer and move it slowly away from her.

(CONTINUED)

6 **Lure her by moving your hand forward** so that she follows it with her whole body. As soon as she's through your legs, say *Good weave* and give her the treat.

7 **Moving slowly, repeat the action with your right leg,** holding a treat in your right hand. Always hold the treat in the same hand as the leg you step forward on and reward her every step. As she learns what you want, you can treat her every few steps.

8 **Once your dog can move back and forth between your legs,** it's time to pick up the pace and make the movement nice and smooth. You may feel like an orchestra conductor with the treat in your moving hand, but it's worth the payoff — this is a really fun trick!

ASK THE VET

Why are dogs so playful?

— Reagan, age 8, Seattle, Washington

Dogs do love to have a good time! This behavior can be traced to their wolf ancestors, or, more specifically, wolf pups. One thing wolf pups love to do is *play*! That's how they learn to hunt. Dog games often mimic aspects of a wolf hunt, such as stalking a toy before pouncing and latching on to it. Or chasing excitedly after a tossed ball that looks like moving prey.

Dogs may like specific toys or types of play based on what they were bred to do. A border collie, for example, is more likely to be a visual player and very keen on following the movement of a toy. A beagle, however, relies on his powerful sense of smell. He may be more interested in play that involves searching out hidden items, such as one of your socks or a tennis ball hidden in the grass.

— Dr. Marty Becker, America's Family Veterinarian, Bonner's Ferry, Idaho

TEACHING BELLY UP

If your dog feels comfortable lying on his back for belly rubs and can consistently perform *Down* on cue, he is ready to learn how to roll over on command, or as I tell Kona, *Belly up!*

1 **Put your dog in a down position facing you.** Kneeling in front of him, hold a treat in your closed hand on one side of your dog's head.

2 **Slowly move the treat back toward his shoulder as you say** ***Belly up.*** As he follows the treat with his nose, your dog should roll over on his side. Praise him and hand over the treat.

3 **Once he is consistently rolling over on his side,** move the hand holding the treat over his shoulder to the other side of his body.

He will have to roll over to keep following the treat with his nose. At first you may need to gently help him completely flip over at first.

4 **As soon he flips over, quickly mark the action by saying** *Good belly up!* and giving him a treat.

When he knows to roll over when you say *Belly up*, you can start to pair the verbal cue with a hand signal of your outstretched hand making a circle in the air so he will perform *Belly up* without you having to say a word.

DiY
Decorated Collars
(for dress-up occasions only)

Glue on a few plastic building blocks or game pieces (use hot glue for best results).

Cut the ends off a fabric belt or an old tie or other tube of fabric. Slip it over the collar and scrunch it up.

Cut an old tie cut in half, slide the collar into the skinnier end, and tie a knot in the fatter end to hang down.

Sew or glue on an assortment of buttons, beads, or other baubles.

Add some pom-poms or a big bow (this collar is an old belt cut down to fit).

TRIVIA
QUIZ 3

1. Why do some dogs bury treats and toys in the backyard or under the sofa cushions?

A. They feel the need to stash extra goodies "for a rainy day."

B. They like the aging odor of treats buried in the ground.

C. They don't want to share their goodies with other dogs.

D. All of the above

2. Which of the following is *not* a reason why dogs yawn?

A. They are stressed by the sound of loud music or the vacuum cleaner.

B. They are tired from playing fetch with you in the backyard.

C. They are excited to see you when you come home from school.

D. They are bored with doing the same trick over and over again.

3. Dogs have reputations for being chow-hounds. Which of the following people food is not safe to give to your dog?

A. Grapes

B. Carrots

C. Apple slices

D. Broiled chicken

4. Why do dogs roll in smelly stuff like poop or a dead animal?

A. As canine camouflage

B. To cover up the scent of flowery pet shampoo

C. Both A and B

D. None of the above

See page 139 for answers.

OUT AND ABOUT
With Your
Four-Legged Pal

Some dogs love being homebodies. But most consider "home" to be anywhere that they can be with *you*! That could be sharing a sofa, taking a hike, or heading out on an adventure in the family car. What matters to your dog is not the zip code, but spending time with you.

So let's set you and your dog up for success when it comes to meeting other dogs, keeping it safe at dog parks, taking terrific road trips, being welcomed at dog-friendly restaurants and hotels, and hosting a dog party worth yapping about.

DOG-TO-DOG INTROS

When you meet another person, either a friend or someone new, you say hello. You may shake hands or give each other high fives. When dogs meet, they don't shake paws. Their version of a doggy handshake is sniffing each other's butt. It may seem rude or disgusting to us, but in the canine world it's good manners.

Well-socialized dogs meeting for the first time or greeting their friends take turns sniffing each other's rear ends to download information about each other. They can tell a lot from doing this: whether the dog is male or female, about how old he is, what he ate at his last meal, what his mood is (happy, sad, or scared), and even how healthy he is. That's pretty amazing, right?

So let your dog be a dog when making new friends, but be aware that being on a leash can make some dogs feel that they have to defend themselves or their human companions. Even if your dog loves making new friends, make sure it's okay to approach any dogs you don't know before getting too close.

ON LEASH. When your dog is on a leash and another person approaches with a friendly dog also on a leash, let them have a chance to do the doggy handshake. Loosen up the leashes so the dogs have room to navigate and sniff each other. Praise them in an upbeat voice for saying hi and then, if you can, have the two dogs walk side by side for a bit to get to know each other more.

I am so **EXCITED!!** Let's play!

Speak, Kona, Speak!

Like me, most dogs love a treat, so when introducing two dogs, it can help to use treats to reward good manners. But always ask before handing out treats to a dog you don't know. Some dogs have food allergies, and others are snappy about snacks. Better to be safe!

FEELING SHY. Let's say your dog appears hesitant or even anxious when approaching other dogs. He will show that by licking his lips, crouching to appear smaller, or even hiding behind your legs. These are all signals to the other dog that your dog is submissive and definitely not wanting to take on the role of lead dog.

In this situation, let the two dogs sit and sniff each other a few feet apart. At the same time, do your best to be calm and upbeat — remember, dogs are experts at downloading our emotions. If you do not act nervous or afraid, your shy or anxious dog will feel a bit safer.

TOO EXCITED. Your dog seems to have an endless supply of energy and joy. He may even start dancing or letting out happy yelps when another leashed dog approaches. Your dog needs you to tone down his enthusiasm before the two dogs get close, especially if the other dog is a senior dog who may not take kindly to such over-the-top hellos.

One trick to try is to use your body to partially block your dog's view of the other dog. Pull out a couple of treats to garner your dog's attention and cue him to *Sit*. If your dog is still too jazzed up, no worries. Smile and acknowledge that your dog is too goofy and energetic to do a sniff-and-greet, then walk quickly by.

READ YOUR DOG

It's sad but true that not all dogs like other dogs. Your dog might have some canine buddies but may act a little aggressive with strange dogs. Or he might be super friendly but not too smart about greeting dogs who aren't as welcoming. Most dogs know how to react when another dog is aggressive, but when you approach another dog and person, play it safe.

Size up how each dog is acting toward the other one before they are close enough to sniff each other. It's okay to avoid meeting by walking in the opposite direction or crossing the street.

A friendly, outgoing dog will show some or all of these behaviors:
* Relaxed body posture
* Happy face with open mouth
* Avoiding direct eye contact with the other dog
* Plopping into a play bow (rear end up, front legs on the ground)
* Wagging his tail gently and loosely

A nervous or aggressive dog will show some or all of these behaviors:
* Licking his lips (a sign of anxiety)
* Tucked-in tail (a sign of fear)
* Hiding behind owner
* Growling
* Stiff body and tight, closed mouth
* Staring directly at the other dog
* Lunging at the other dog

SIZING UP A DOG PARK

Do you love recess at school? Do you love spending time at the playground where you can glide down the slide and go back and forth on the swings? Fun, right? Well, some dogs love to romp in their own type of playground called a dog park.

Dog parks are fenced-in areas with double-gated door entries where dogs can be off leash while they explore, run, and romp with other dogs.

Be your dog's best friend by exercising some caution before entering a dog park. There should be rules posted, so read those first, then look and listen.

SIGNS OF A GOOD DOG PARK:
* Dogs barking happily
* Dogs playing nicely with one another
* Plenty of room for dogs to break away from the action
* People watching or playing with their dogs
* Grass or other nice footing (not pavement or dusty dirt)

SIGNS OF A BAD DOG PARK:
* Dogs growling or yelping
* Dogs aggressively chasing scared dogs
* Too many dogs for the space
* People reading or using their phones instead of paying attention to their dogs
* Toddlers playing inside the fence, especially if they have food in their hands

Some dogs aren't fans of dog parks — and that's okay. Your mission is to focus on your dog's body language as you get near the gate of the dog park. Do not force her to go inside if she is pulling back on the leash, whining, or crouching. She's telling you she doesn't feel safe to enter. Instead, go with plan B: take her on a fun, brisk leashed walk away from the dog park.

A little help with this, please?

Speak, Kona, Speak!

I love making new friends at the dog park. One reason I get to go is because Arden knows I'll come when she calls my name — even if I am playing with a goofy boxer! Please make sure your dog has a good recall before hitting a dog park. You don't want distractions getting in the way of him racing back to you.

ROAD TRIP TIME!

All you have to do is utter the words "Want to go . . .?" and most dogs will wag their tails in high gear and leap with delight at the invitation to join you and your family in the car. They don't care if you're just going to the store.

Here are some tips to keep your dog safe in the car, whether you're traveling a few blocks or across the country.

BUILD UP YOUR DOG'S TRAVEL ENDURANCE. With a puppy or newly adopted dog, set him up for success by taking short trips of less than 10 minutes. Gradually work up to longer trips.

KEEP YOUR DOG SECURE IN THE CAR. If your dog can travel in his crate, great! (For more about crates, see page 46.) Otherwise, have him wear a pet safety harness that attaches to the seat belt. He should ride in the back seat or the sectioned-off back area of an SUV or station wagon. Always clip your dog's leash to the harness when he's in the car and keep hold of the leash as you unclip him before leaving the car. This is a good opportunity to reinforce the *Sit* and *Stay* commands.

PROVIDE PROPER ID. Your dog should sport a collar with identification tags that include your family's phone number. And speak with your vet about getting an "invisible" ID — a microchip. The microchip is a tiny object about the size of a grain of rice that a veterinarian inserts in your dog's shoulder area (a quick process that feels the same as an injection). The microchip contains your dog's name and your family's and veterinarian's contact information. If you and your dog are separated somehow and he is picked up as a stray, most veterinary clinics and shelters have a scanner that will read the microchip, greatly increasing the odds that you'll be reunited.

PACK A FEW ESSENTIALS. For short or long trips, always bring a spare leash, extra doggy poop bags, water for you and your dog, and a small bag of treats.

DINING WITH YOUR DOG

More and more restaurants are opening up to dogs these days. Whether you have a dog-friendly place near you or you find one while traveling, you'll only be welcome if your dog brings her best manners to the table. Bring your dog only if you know she shines in social settings — and you can't expect her to know how to behave if you haven't practiced at home. Here are tips to make the dining experience pleasant for all patrons.

EXERCISE YOUR DOG FIRST. To increase the chances that your canine companion mellows out while you enjoy a meal, take her out for a brisk walk before heading to the restaurant. Burning off energy will make her more apt to nap under the table.

Speak, Kona, Speak!

I am no longer surprised when strangers greet me by saying, "Hi, Kona." That's because Arden had my name and her cell phone number embroidered in bright yellow on my red collar. That makes it easy for anyone to know my name and how to get hold of Arden in case I get lost. Paws up for a good idea!

SCOPE OUT THE SCENE. Request a table in a corner or away from the entrance to minimize opportunities for your dog to bark or try to sniff other patrons and their dogs. On sunny days, find a table that offers shade, and bring a water bowl.

REIN IN YOUR DOG. To prevent your four-legged friend from bothering patrons at neighboring tables, keep her on a short leash. Periodically reward her for lying quietly. Don't expect her to patiently spend hours under the table, though.

MAKE A SPLASH

Some dogs love water, whether it's a pool, a lake, or the ocean. If your dog loves to do the dog paddle, ride in a boat or kayak, or even surf, that is way cool! Heed these water safety tips to ensure that your water time is fun *and* safe.

IF YOU HAVE A POOL, TEACH YOUR DOG how to safely enter and exit it. Start with water play in the shallow end and teach him that this is his "safety spot" for getting out of the pool. If your pool doesn't have wide, shallow steps, ask your parents about investing in a floatable doggy ramp.

BE YOUR DOG'S LIFEGUARD. Never let your dog in your pool without supervision, and make sure your pool has a dog-proof gate to block access when you're not around. Take a pet first-aid class. Learn how to perform doggy CPR and rescue breathing, and what to do if your dog is drowning.

ALL DOGS CAN SWIM. Dogs who have challenges in learning how to dog paddle include those with short legs and long backs (corgis and dachshunds), barrel-chested dogs (bulldogs), and dogs with short snouts (pugs). For a dog like this who wants to swim, fit

him with a canine life vest that helps him stay afloat. Support your dog's belly when he is getting the hang of paddling, then stay near him as he builds up his swimming confidence.

ALWAYS PUT A LIFE VEST ON ANY DOG, even a good swimmer, who is joining you on a boat, kayak, or canoe.

PROTECT YOUR POOCH FROM THE SUN. Before swim time, dab dog-safe sunscreen on the top of the nose (not the wet part!) and bare belly to reduce the risk of sunburn. The sunscreen needs to be waterproof, quick drying, and nongreasy.

END THE WATER PLAY BEFORE your dog becomes overtired. Some dogs love the water so much or are so eager to fetch sticks that they won't stop on their own. A tired dog who is panting heavily while swimming may get water in his lungs or swallow enough water to make himself vomit.

LET YOUR DOG PLAY ONLY IN CLEAN WATER. Dirty, muddy, or scummy water might have parasites that can cause an infection called giardia as well as doggy diarrhea. Keep him away from water that smells bad or is thick with algae.

HIKE THIS WAY, DOGGY!

If you and your family like to take walks on nature trails, your canine chum will surely want to join your adventures. Just be sure she is strong enough to complete a long hike. Smaller dogs need to take more steps than larger dogs and may tire more quickly.

BE PREPARED. Bring plenty of water, a collapsible bowl, people and dog snacks, a first-aid kit, and spare poop bags. Pick a trail that allows dogs and follow the trail rules (some allow dogs to be off leash while others require them to be leashed at all times).

Don't forget appropriate flea and tick protection. You don't want your pup "bugged" while hiking. (See the next chapter for more on the importance of good health care.)

HAVE PROPER EQUIPMENT. Before you go, make sure your dog is sporting a collar with identification and wearing a bright-colored, reflective harness. A harness is far safer than a collar for a hiking dog, no matter the dog's size. You have more control by attaching the leash to the D ring on the harness. Play it safe by avoiding those zipline-like retractable leashes with bulky plastic handles — the line can snap, and your dog can get too far ahead of you to be under your control.

SET YOUR PUP UP FOR SUCCESS. Before you hit the trail, be sure your dog can do the following:

Walk nicely on a leash without yanking and pulling. Some trails can be rocky, and you don't want to fall because your dog suddenly pulls on the leash.

Come quickly to you each and every time you call her. Practice her recall in a fenced-in area. Then put her on a long lead in an unfenced area to test her ability to race back to you when you call her name.

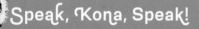

Speak, Kona, Speak!

If you forget to bring a water bowl for your thirsty dog, you can make one out of a spare poop bag. Or pour water into your baseball hat or your cupped hands. Ah! I feel refreshed already!

STAYING AT A DOG-FRIENDLY HOTEL

If your dog loves to travel and is well behaved, consider bringing him on a family vacation that includes staying at a dog-friendly hotel. These tips for traveling with a canine companion will make your trip more fun for everyone.

BRING FAMILIAR CHOW. To minimize any chance of diarrhea or stomach upset, stick with your dog's regular food and favorite healthy treats. Pack bottled water or bring a gallon jug of water from your home faucet. Bring water and food bowls. Offer water at each stop.

PACK PET AMENITIES. To help your dog feel more at home inside the hotel room, be sure to bring familiar items bearing his scent, such as his bed or crate and definitely his favorite toy.

FOLLOW THE HOTEL RULES. Many dog-friendly hotels stand by one big rule: Dogs are not allowed to be left alone in the hotel room. That's because they may engage in nuisance barking or be so nervous or bored that they wreck the room.

LOCATE PET-CARE SERVICES. Call ahead to ask the hotel staff about local pet sitters or doggy day cares that can care for your dog while you and your family are out and about at places where dogs aren't welcome.

Kona's "Pet-iquette" for Hotel Stays

I love joining Arden and my feline brother, Casey, on road trips. We often spend the night at a pet-friendly hotel, so I know all about being a good guest. This is our checklist for checking in:

* Bring a sheet or blanket from home to place on top of the bedspread if your pet sleeps on the bed with you.

* Bring a couple of your dog's favorite toys — but not one with a loud squeaker that might irritate the guests in the next room.

* Pack paper towels and an enzyme-based cleaner to mop up accidents.

* Store your dog's favorite treats and food in sealed containers. Serve meals in the bathroom, not on the carpeted floor. Keep the toilet lid down.

* Hang a Do Not Disturb sign on the doorknob to prevent an unexpected visit by housekeeping staff.

IT'S TIME TO PAW-TY!

Most dogs love to socialize, so why not celebrate a special occasion by hosting a dog party? You could break out the invitations for any of these reasons:

* Adoption anniversary
* Your dog's birthday
* Basic obedience graduation
* Fund-raiser for local animal shelter
* Halloween costume contest
* Get-together with dog park pals
* Why not? (You don't really need a reason!)

Dog parties are terrific opportunities to practice canine manners in a fun atmosphere, but they can present a challenge. Some dogs may forget their training in a new or very distracting setting. Fortunately, you can make sure all your guests have a good time. Your goal is to make this a party with a purpose: to polish your dog's mastery of obedience commands and good manners while showcasing some cool canine capers.

To host a successful dog party, consider these guidelines.

SET A BUDGET. How much money do you have? How much of it are you willing to spend on your pet?

FIGURE OUT THE GUEST LIST. Determine the number by the sociability of the dogs, how many people will be helping you supervise, and the size of the party location. Maybe just a few doggy guests for inside the house or backyard but up to 10 or 12 if the party is at a dog-friendly place, such as an indoor dog center.

SET A DATE. For an informal party in your backyard, you can plan a party in just a few days. If you want to reserve a place, you may need to book the space in advance.

BE CLEAR ON THE INVITATION. Whether you send a card in the mail or invite guests by text, telephone, e-mail, or social media, make sure to include the date, the start and stop times, the reason for the event, and the location. Two hours is a good time frame. Ask people to RSVP. And find out in advance if any doggy guests have food allergies before you select the treats or canine cake to serve.

AT THE PARTY

For a party in your backyard, mark out different zones for food serving, game playing, and doggy bathrooms.

* Make a plan for the lineup of activities, but don't try to cram too much into one event.
* Always keep dogs on leashes and spread apart when doling out slices of doggy cake or treats to avoid any food fights.
* If you wish to give party gifts to your attendees, save time at the end of the party to hand them out.

Speak, Kona, Speak!

Just like you, I love hanging out with my BFFs — that's best furry friends. My big sister, Bujeau, is a lot bigger than me, but we have a great time going on long walks together.

I also love playing with my canine cousin, Oliver, an energetic 20-pound schnoodle. We chase each other all over the yard, yipping and yapping the whole time. Then we head inside, slurp up some water, and plop on the same dog bed to recharge for another romp.

Bujeau and Oliver definitely top the list of guests for any special event Arden and I host.

GRRR-EAT GAMES

At the heart of any good dog fete are the creative games. The following popular games can be played indoors or outdoors.

SNOOPY SAYS

This canine version of Simon Says is designed to hone doggy manners in a party setting. To set it up, have your guests line up with their dogs on leashes. Make sure that there is ample space between each person-dog team.

RULES: Each team must comply with your command whenever you say, "Snoopy says." For example, if you say, "Snoopy says, sit your dog," people must ask their dogs to sit. But if you simply say, "Sit your dog," any team who does so must head to the sidelines. Teams are also eliminated when they fail to perform a "Snoopy says" command.

THE WINNER: The final team left who has heeded all the "Snoopy says" commands.

CANINE WILLPOWER

Here's a fun way to reinforce the *Stay* command. This party game tests the willpower of chowhounds. Before starting, cut up several hot dogs into one-inch chunks. You'll need two or three pieces for each guest.

RULES: Line the guests up about three feet apart with their leashed dogs in down position. On the count of three, have each person say *Stay* and then place a piece of hot dog about a foot from their dog's nose. Contestants are not allowed to touch their dogs or yank back on their leashes.

THE WINNER: The dog who resists temptation the longest and waits until her person gives her the *Okay* sign to eat the treat.

CANINE MUSICAL CHAIRS

This game rewards dogs who walk nicely by your side on a leash and plop promptly into a sit. You'll need a source of music and some hula hoops or lengths of rope to make circles. Place the hoops or rope circles on the floor in a row with plenty of space between them. There should be one fewer circle than the total number of teams.

RULES: Line up the teams on one side of the row. Instruct the teams to move in one direction around the line of hoops when the music starts. As soon as the music stops, each person must put one foot in the circle and get their dog to sit down inside the circle. The dog-person team unable to reach a circle is eliminated. Remove one circle after each round.

THE WINNER: The last team to successfully claim a circle.

DiY

A Doggy Piñata

Your guests will be delighted when a cascade of biscuits falls from this custom-made piñata. This fun activity should only be presented to dogs who know one other and are not likely to get into a food fight.

Cardboard box

Strong scissors or utility knife

Heavy tape and cellophane tape

Glue, glue gun, or glue stick

Tissue paper, crepe paper, and poster board or colored paper

Sturdy string

Small dog biscuits and treats

1 MAKE THE HOUSE

A Cut off two opposite bottom flaps. Save one of the flap pieces to make the pull tab.

B Fold two of the top flaps together to form the roof peak. Tape the flaps together with plenty of heavy tape.

C Trace the outline of the roof peak on the remaining flaps. Trim off the extra cardboard.

2 MAKE THE PULL TAB

A Punch a hole in the center of the cut-off flap piece you saved from the bottom of the box.

B Cut a piece of string about 2 feet long. Tie a big knot in one end and thread it through the hole in the flap. Reinforce the hole with tape.

C Securely tie a dog biscuit to the other end of the string.

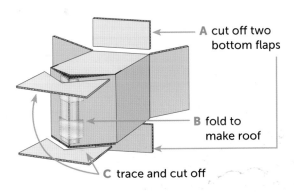

A cut off two bottom flaps

B fold to make roof

C trace and cut off

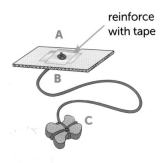

reinforce with tape

A

B

C

3 DECORATE AND FILL

A The possibilities are endless! We layered strips of crepe paper and tissue paper to cover the sides of the box and made a door from colored paper.

B Carefully pulling open the flaps on either side of the roof, run a long piece of string through the box. Tie the ends in a strong knot.

C Set the box on its side and put a handful or two of treats inside. Fold the two bottom flaps almost shut.

D Insert the pull tab between the bottom flaps, lining it up to cover the opening so the treats won't fall out. Tape the flaps together with cellophane tape.
    Experiment to find the right amount of tape to hold the weight of the treats while still letting the flaps open with a tug on the pull tab.

4 HANG AND FINISH

A Cut the roof from poster board or colored paper. Make it a little wider and longer than the box, so it hangs over the sides. Fold it in half and cut small slits at each edge of the fold for the string.

B Hang the piñata just higher than your dog's head — you want him to jump up and grab the biscuit. This will cause the pull tab to yank open the flaps and release the treats!

C Slide the roof on, fitting the string into the slits.

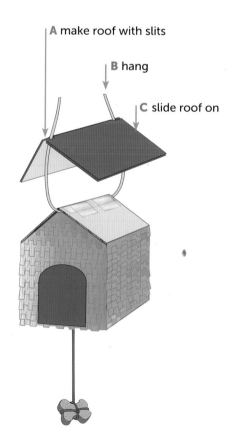

A make roof with slits

B hang

C slide roof on

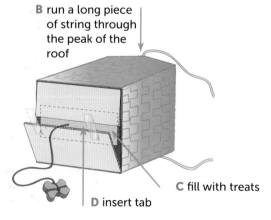

B run a long piece of string through the peak of the roof

C fill with treats

D insert tab

SOME OTHER IDEAS

POSTER BOARD

Cut two poster board shapes. Glue them to a cardboard food box with a tab-in-slot top.

A MAILING TUBE

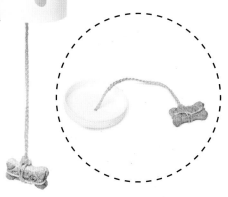

Decorate a mailing tube and fill it with treats. Hang one treat from the cap of the tube as bait.

1 To hang, run a piece of ribbon through the bottom of the box.

2 Fill the box with treats.

3 Loop string through the top flaps and close the flaps with the tab.

Bow Wow Brownies

Your canine party guests will howl with delight when you dish up these bark-a-licious brownies. Don't worry — these dog-safe treats don't contain a lick of chocolate.

½ cup vegetable oil

2 tablespoons honey

1 cup whole-wheat flour

½ cup carob chips

¼ cup carob powder

4 eggs

1 teaspoon vanilla extract

1 teaspoon baking powder

1 Preheat the oven to 350°F (180°C). Spray a 9 × 13-inch baking pan with cooking spray.

2 Using a wooden spoon, blend the oil and honey thoroughly in a medium bowl.

3 Add the flour, carob chips, carob powder, eggs, vanilla, and baking powder, and mix well.

4 Spread the batter in the pre-pared baking pan and bake for 30 to 35 minutes. Test for done-ness by inserting a toothpick into the center. If it comes out dry, the brownies are ready.

5 Let cool in the pan, then frost (see recipe on the facing page).

6 Cut into bite-sized squares about 1 inch by 1 inch. Store extras in a sealed container in the refrigerator.

Serving size is 1 or 2 squares for dogs under 30 pounds; 2 to 4 for dogs above 30 pounds.

Bow Wow Brownie Frosting

12 ounces fat-free cream cheese

1 teaspoon vanilla extract

1 teaspoon honey

1 Blend the cream cheese, vanilla, and honey in a small electric mixer.

2 Spread the frosting over the pan of cooled brownies with a spatula. Don't forget to lick the bowl!

Marvelous Mutt Meatballs

Dogs dig meaty treats. Here is a fun recipe to make for special occasions like your dog's birthday or adoption anniversary date.

½ pound ground beef or turkey

½ cup breadcrumbs

½ cup grated cheddar cheese

1 carrot, shredded

1 egg, whisked

3 tablespoons low-sodium tomato paste

1 Preheat the oven to 350°F (180°C). Spray a baking sheet with cooking spray or line it with parchment paper.

2 Stir all the ingredients in a large mixing bowl until well blended.

3 Roll the mix by the spoonful into mini meatballs.

4 Place the meatballs on the prepared baking sheet and bake for 15 to 20 minutes, or until the meatballs are no longer pink inside.

5 Cool on the baking sheet and store in a sealed container in the refrigerator.

Serving size is 1 meatball for dogs under 30 pounds; 2 meatballs for dogs above 30 pounds.

BE YOUR DOG'S
Best Health Ally

Having a dog means you play many roles: feeder, poop-picker-upper, daily walker, and favorite playmate. That last one is important, because playing with your dog is one of the best ways to keep him from getting too fat or having so much pent-up energy that he gets into trouble. He needs regular walks, but you can also burn up energy and calories by playing canine games, no matter what the weather. Try to find time for a couple of short play sessions every day.

This chapter offers fun ways to exercise your dog as well as information on everyday health and tips on visiting the vet.

HEAD OUTDOORS FOR K9 GAMES

When the weather is nice, usher your dog outside for four of Kona's favorite games: I hide, you seek; canine scavenger hunt; fetch some fun; safe tug-of-war. (All of these games can be adapted to play indoors, too.)

I HIDE, YOU SEEK

This is a great game to reinforce your dog's command of the *Come* cue. Have someone hang on to your dog as you dash out of sight and find a hiding spot. When in position (like behind a tree or shed), call your dog's name and say *Come* once. Then be still. Let him work his nose and brain to sniff you out. Praise and treat.

CANINE SCAVENGER HUNT

Does your clever canine know the names of his various toys? Kona knows that "Foxy" is the orange stuffed toy and "Squirrel" is the gray-black stuffed toy in her toy bin. This game will exercise your dog's brain and muscle while increasing his vocabulary.

Start by spending a few minutes each day showing your dog one of his favorite toys while saying its name, like "Here's Foxy" or "This is Squirrel." Encourage your dog to sniff at and play with the toy. Keep saying that toy's name as your dog plays. Play fetch or hide-and-seek with the toy while saying *Find* or *Bring me* with the name of the toy. Stick with one toy for a few days to ensure your dog is associating the spoken name with the toy. Then you can gradually introduce another one.

After you've introduced the names of two toys, test your dog's understanding by putting the toys a couple of feet apart and asking him to bring you one of them. Lavish him with praise for choosing the right one. Once he is consistently picking between two toys, you can introduce others one at a time.

To move the game outside, stash a few of the favorite toys behind trees or in other spots around your yard or in a park. Then have your dog (leashed or unleashed, depending on the safety of the situation) go on a search mission to find the items.

FETCH SOME FUN

Most dogs love to chase moving objects, especially balls or flying discs. This is a super way to exercise your dog. Some dogs love chasing after the ball or disc but won't give it back. You need to teach your dog all the steps in fetching: *Chase*, *Retrieve*, and *Drop it*.

To teach a dog to bring an object back to you, start with two identical balls or discs. When your dog has retrieved the first one but won't give it up, call him to you and throw the other one. He'll likely drop the first object to go after the second.

When he does, pick up the first object and repeat the switch. Once he learns that you will always throw another ball or disc, start saying the command *Drop it* before you throw the next object. Once he lets go of the toy, pick it up and hand him a treat or throw the same object. He will soon learn it is worth it to give up the ball or disc for a tasty treat or the chance to play more fetch.

Speak, Kona, Speak!

I confess that the first few times Arden tossed a soft flying disc for me to catch, it bonked me on the head. I was clumsy. And your dog may be, too, in the beginning. But that's okay. Just be patient and start with short throwing distances so your dog can hone her eye-mouth coordination. Be sure to let out a happy *Good catch* to your dog to encourage and motivate her. Now I can drop the disc at Arden's feet and start sprinting ahead as she releases it for me to leap in the air and catch it. I love, love, love this backyard game!

Dogs, just like kids, can get a little stir-crazy staying inside during winter. When the ground is covered with snow, vary your game by playing snowball fetch. Make a batch of snowballs to toss for your dog to chase after and try to catch. Many dogs love to pounce and dig in the snow.

SAFE TUG-OF-WAR

Choose a sturdy tug toy that is at least three feet in length to give a safe distance between your hand and your dog's mouth. Tell your dog to *Sit* and *Stay* as you drag the tug toy in front of him. If he grabs the toy, tell him *Drop it* and give him a treat for complying. Give him permission to pick up the toy by saying *Take it.* Let him tug for 10 to 15 seconds, then give the *Drop it* cue. Make him wait until you say *Take it* before starting the game again.

It's important to teach your dog that you start and end all tugging sessions and that you'll stop playing if he pulls too hard or doesn't heed your *Drop it* command.

119

FUN AND GAMES
IN THE HOUSE

Even when Old Man Winter dumps snow or it is raining cats and dogs, keeping your dog fit is a year-round commitment. Here are some fun ways to burn up energy if you have to stay inside because of nasty weather.

MINI OBSTACLE COURSE.
Mix and match these obstacles to challenge your dog's interest and keep her moving.

* With your dog on a short lead, weave between a line of objects, like paper plates, books, or small pillows, in a large open space.
* Balance a broom on two piles of books or a couple of large cans and encourage your dog to hop over it.
* Hold a hula hoop a few inches off the ground and lure her through it.

AEROBIC ACTION. This game requires another person and a handful of treats. Stand at the opposite ends of a long hallway or at the top and bottom of a staircase. Start with your dog sitting next to one of you. The other person calls the dog in a happy upbeat tone, rewarding her when she races to get the treat. A few minutes of running back and forth will give your dog a good workout.

MIXED-UP CUES. String together the cues *Sit* and then *Down* several times in a row to have your dog perform a succession of "puppy pushups." Or string together a bunch of different cues in row, like *Sit, Stay, Come, Down, Sit, Belly up!*

A rainy day is also a good opportunity to practice the all-important *Stay* cue by gradually increasing the length of time she must stay in place. Heap on praise and dole out occasional treats when she does well.

IS THERE A VET IN THE HOUSE?

One of the most important roles you can take on is playing health detective for your dog.

How? Easy. Just be on the lookout for any clues that may indicate your dog is not her usual healthy self — then let your parents know. The sooner you can spot problems in your dog, the sooner she can get help. That requires you to tap into various pet detective skills: observing, smelling, hearing, and touching.

Let's say your dog or pup is usually full of energy. But one day, she wants to stay in her bed or declines your invitation to play fetch. Or maybe your dog is usually a chowhound but at mealtime, she sniffs the bowl and walks away. Or perhaps she is itching a lot or chewing on her paws. Or you notice she has a bump on her back or a red rash on her belly that wasn't there a week ago.

These are all clues telling you that something is wrong.

LEARN PET FIRST AID

One of the best ways to show your dog just how much you love her is to take a pet first-aid class. Kids are welcome to join their parents at these classes. Here are three reasons why you should learn pet first aid:

* You will learn how to stay calm and focused when your dog is ill or injured.
* You will help your family save money on veterinary bills by catching your dog's health issues early.
* You will learn what to do in a pet emergency to possibly save your dog's life.

By taking a class, you will learn how to help a dog who is choking, how to bandage a bloody paw, how to give medicine, how to perform rescue breathing and CPR (cardiopulmonary resuscitation), and much, much more!

CHECK YOUR DOG FROM NOSE TO TAIL

Schedule a time each week to perform a head-to-tail wellness checkup. This is a great way to bond with your dog while you look for possible health issues.

Before you begin, draw three outlines of your dog: side view, belly view, and head view. You will use these drawings to mark places where your dog may have a problem like cuts, bumps, or rashes to point out to your parents and your veterinarian.

Pick a small room that is free of distractions and a door that you can close. Maybe you can usher your dog into your bedroom or lure her into the bathroom with a treat. Turn the page to learn how to conduct your exam.

Speak, Kona, Speak

You can be a good health ally by thinking pink! That's because gum color is an important sign of good health. Think of it like this: healthy gums look like bubblegum! (Not that dogs should ever chew gum, of course.)

When Arden gently lifts my upper lip to demonstrate to our students how to check gums, I'm proud to show off my white teeth and healthy pink gums. If your dog's gums are white, gray, blue, bright red, or yellow, something is wrong. Tell your parents immediately so that they can contact your veterinarian.

THE WELLNESS CHECKUP

Use the outline pictures of your dog (see previous page) to mark any findings. Share concerns with your parents. Always finish your at-home wellness exam with lots of praise for your dog!

Start at your dog's head. Feel her nose. A healthy nose is dry or slightly moist. An unhealthy nose is extremely dry or full of mucus — yuck!

Gently fold back each ear to look inside. Give a sniff, too. If you see dark brown dirt that looks like coffee grounds or smell something like dirty socks, she may have ear mites or an ear infection.

Hold a treat in front of her eyes and slowly move it from left to right to check if her eyes track the movement. Are the pupils in her eyes the same size? If one pupil is smaller or bigger than the other, it could be a medical problem. The follow-the-treat trick also helps you determine if your dog has any stiffness in her neck.

Check her belly for redness or rashes. Feel for lumps or bumps.

Glide your hand from her head to the base of her tail. Then slowly and gently massage her whole body. Be on the lookout for any wincing or resistance that may indicate a sore muscle or arthritis.

Examine each paw for any cuts, overgrown nails, or ticks. (Ugh, ticks like to hide between toes!)

Gently lift her tail to see if there is any redness on her anus or dry poop dangling. If you've noticed her scooting across the floor on her rear end, she might have worms.

Check her tail for any cuts or bumps. There are a lot of tiny bones in the tail, and a dog can injure it by wagging too hard and hitting something!

DECODE THE THREE Ps: POOP, PEE, AND PUKE

Poop happens. So does pee and sometimes even puke. You can catch some health concerns early by paying attention to your dog's "deposits."

POOP FIRST

Let's start with poop, or feces. Normal, healthy dog poop should be chocolate brown in color, the shape of a log, easy to pick up (with a poop bag), and slightly squishy. If your dog is pooping small, hard pellets, he may be suffering from constipation. If he is squirting watery, reddish brown puddles, he has diarrhea.

If your dog's poop really stinks and you spot what looks like coffee grounds, it could signal your dog has internal bleeding. This warrants a veterinary exam pronto!

SPOTLIGHT ON URINE

Urine tells a lot about your dog's health. Normal dog urine should be yellow and not have a strong odor. Brown, orange, pink, or red urine indicates a health issue. To determine the color, use a white paper towel. For a female dog, put the paper under her just before she gets ready to squat and urinate outdoors. For a male dog, time the paper towel test to catch some spray as soon as he stops and starts to lift a hind leg.

Report any changes in how often your dog urinates and how much.

Speak, Kona, Speak!

Doggy diarrhea is no picnic and neither is constipation. Fortunately, there's a yummy solution. Whenever my tummy is upset, Arden adds a tablespoon of canned pumpkin in my food bowl for a few meals and my poop is soon perfect again. Kids, make sure to choose plain unsweetened pumpkin purée, not the sugar-filled pumpkin pie filling. Paws up for pumpkin power!

For example, if your dog has always been good about going to the bathroom outside and is suddenly peeing on the living room rug, something is wrong. And if your dog releases only a few drops of urine while squatting, he could have a blockage in his urinary tract. This is a medical emergency!

WHY DOGS VOMIT

Dogs vomit for many reasons. Topping the list is an upset tummy from eating spoiled food, eating too quickly, accidentally ingesting poison from a plant or medication, or being carsick.

Yes, vomit is yucky, but put your pet detective skills to use. If your dog vomits once in a great while and then goes back about his normal routine, don't worry. But if he vomits more than once in a day, acts sluggish, and turns down any food offerings, he should be examined by your veterinarian. Play it safe — for your dog's sake!

Find Your Dog's Heartbeat

Your dog's heart is located on his chest between his front legs. Place your palm on that spot and you will feel his heart go thump-thump-thump. At your dog's next checkup, ask your veterinarian if you can listen to your dog's heartbeat using the stethoscope. Way cool, right?

A healthy dog's heart beats 60 to 140 times per minute, depending on the size of the dog. Small dogs have faster heartbeats than big dogs. A Chihuahua's healthy heart rate is 100 to 140 beats per minute. A big Labrador retriever has a healthy heart rate of 60 to 100 beats per minute.

ASK THE VET

How can a dog still walk if he loses one of his legs?

— Jackson, age 6, Dallas, Texas

Sometimes a leg is so badly injured or infected that it needs to be removed. When this happens to a person, he or she usually learns to walk with an artificial leg (called a prosthesis). If only part of the leg has to be removed, sometimes dogs get protheses, too.

When a dog loses a whole leg, though, he still has three left. Most of these "tripod" dogs adapt very well, although it may take them a little longer to stand up. They hop with one leg while walking or running with the other two. Most of the time they can move around just as quickly as a dog with four legs.

Some dogs who lose the use of their hind legs learn to move around in a wheeled cart. The great thing about dogs is they always seem to make the best of a bad situation.

— Dr. Michael LoSasso, Frisco Emergency Pet Care, Frisco, Texas

MAKE VET VISITS LESS SCARY

Even though veterinarians love dogs, dogs don't always love them. A trip to the vet is often a scary experience, and your dog might not be on her best behavior. You can do your part to help make veterinary visits less frightening for your dog with the following tips.

USE THE SAFE SPACE OF A CARRIER. If your small dog is used to staying in a crate, put her in a carrier to transport her in the car and into the veterinary clinic. This is not only safer all around, but it makes your furry friend feel more secure while you both wait for her appointment.

Accustom her to the carrier beforehand by keeping it out in the open and tossing treats inside for her to sniff out. That way she won't associate it only with going to the vet. (For more on crate training, see page 46.)

BUCKLE UP A BIGGER DOG. You don't go anywhere without safety restraints, and neither should your dog. If your dog isn't riding in a carrier or crate, make sure she is used to being buckled into a safety harness on every trip. It's the safest way to travel, and if your dog is used to going lots places in the car, instead of just to the vet, she won't panic and make things worse when you do have to take her.

GO ON A TEST RUN. Ask your parents if you can bring your dog to the veterinary clinic for a short visit to receive treats and happy attention from the veterinarian and staff. Leave after a few minutes. Repeat a few times over the span of several months. Your dog will start viewing the vet clinic as a welcoming place.

KEEP YOUR DOG BY YOUR SIDE. While in the waiting room, keep your dog near you and not too close to other pets. Give her plenty of space, especially from dogs in grouchy moods. Have your dog face you to help keep her calm.

SPEAK IN A CALM, HAPPY VOICE. Never use baby talk with your scared dog. Dogs read our moods very well, and you need to convey that all is well. In a dog's mind, a person talking baby talk is not confident or in control of a situation. Baby talk can actually cause some dogs to panic and become stressed or scared.

SKIP THE STRESS. If your dog is very nervous or overexcited, ask if you can be ushered right into the exam room or wait in the car until the veterinarian is ready to see you.

TRY A FEW TREATS. Ask the veterinarian or staff member if you can bring treats to give your dog in the exam room to distract her while being examined by the vet staff and veterinarian. Be respectful of what the vet says. Sometimes the best thing is for the owner to leave during a stressful procedure, like having blood drawn. That way, you can be the good guy who comforts her afterward.

CHOOSE FEAR FREE HANDLING

More and more veterinarians recognize that some dogs are downright afraid to enter the clinic lobby or to be examined. Instead of trying to wrestle or restrain these dogs, many veterinarians are now using safer, gentler handling techniques when greeting and treating dogs. They are becoming certified in Fear Free handling techniques designed to reduce fear, stress, and anxiety in pets as well as generate more accurate and thorough examinations.

For example, during an exam, a small dog may be placed on a cushioned bedding on the exam table to prevent her from slipping on the stainless steel. Before a dog is vaccinated, the veterinarian may gently give therapeutic massages up and down the dog's body as a veterinary technician distracts the dog by offering a treat when the injection is done.

ASK THE VET

Why do I need to brush my dog's teeth?

— Cohen, age 11, Davenport, Iowa

If you didn't brush your teeth, you would develop cavities, bad breath, and gum disease, and eventually you would lose your teeth. While dogs don't usually get cavities, not brushing their teeth can result in similar dental problems. Here is how to keep your dog's teeth healthy:

* Get the correct toothbrush. Your toothbrush is not good for your pet. He needs one with a longer handle and a tilted head that will fit into the mouth. For smaller dogs, a finger toothbrush is good.
* Use a pet-appropriate toothpaste because your toothpaste can make pets sick.
* Be patient and gentle with brushing.

* Follow up with your veterinarian yearly for examinations and deep cleaning.

So get the right toothbrush and toothpaste, and start taking care of your pet's teeth. Remember, you want your dog to learn to enjoy the experience while you help him keep his teeth clean.

— Dr. Debora Charles, Casa Linda Animal Clinic, Dallas, Texas

WHEN TO TAKE YOUR DOG TO THE VET

Beyond the obvious situation like a broken bone, heavy bleeding, or massive trauma to the head, abdomen, or chest, there are other scenarios that merit a prompt trip to the veterinarian. Here are some of them:

* Being unable to walk.
* Having difficulty breathing.
* Falling from a height of several feet or down a flight of stairs.
* Suffering a deep cut, bite, or puncture wound.
* Eating poison, such as rat bait, car antifreeze, or human medicine.
* Swelling of stomach; drooling but unable to vomit. This could be bloat, a life-threatening condition that strikes deep-chested dogs who eat food quickly.
* Collapsing and passing out.
* Having a first-time seizure or a prolonged episode.
* Being bitten by a snake.

Cooling Down a Hot Dog

Dogs normally pant when they are warm or exercising, but a dog who is becoming way too hot will pant very heavily and quickly. He will also sweat through his paw pads, and his gums will turn bright red. Taken together, these are signs of heat stroke, which is very serious.

Immediately usher your dog to a shady place. Place his paws one at a time in cool water. If you can, place a cool wet towel on his belly. Remove it every few minutes and add more cool water. Don't use ice water and ice cubes; that can cause shock.

DiY
Pet First-Aid Kit

It's a good idea to have a first-aid kit in the house for your family. You should also have one for your dog. Some of the items are the same, but this way you'll know that everything in the kit is only for animal use. Post this number on the kit or in a handy place: ASPCA Poison Control (1-800-426-4435).

Gauze pads and a roll of gauze (for cuts, bleeding wounds, and mild burns)

Instant cold compress (to reduce swelling)

First-aid tape (to keep bandages in place)

Blunt-tipped scissors (to cut adhesive tape or gauze)

Alcohol swabs (to clean a wound or sterilize a tool)

Antibiotic ointment (to disinfect a wound)

A roll of **self-cling stretchy bandage,** also called vet wrap (to prevent the dog from pawing or biting off bandages)

Pet-safe antihistamine gels (to treat an insect bite or sting)

Styptic powder (to stop minor bleeding)

Sting relief pads (to treat an insect bite or sting)

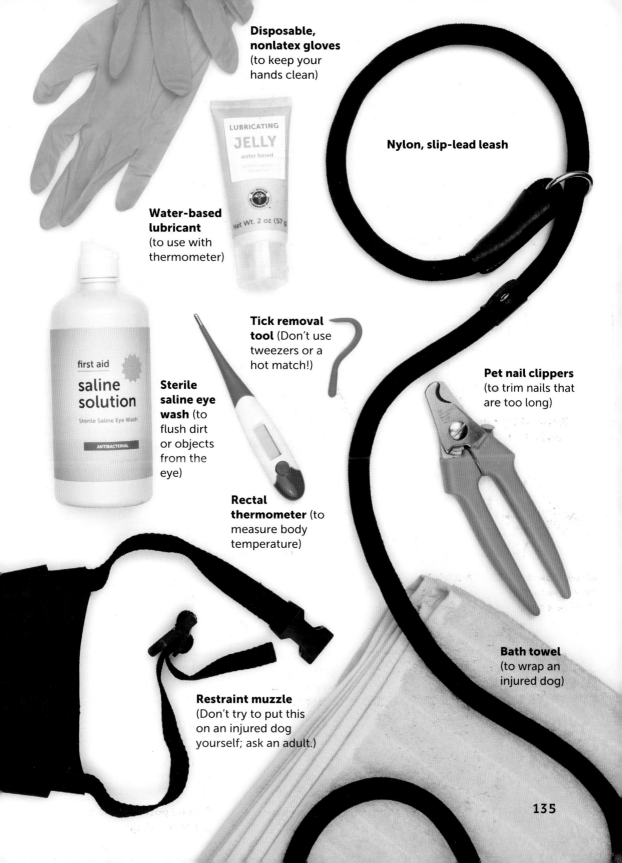

Disposable, nonlatex gloves (to keep your hands clean)

LUBRICATING **JELLY** water based Net Wt. 2 oz (57 g)

Water-based lubricant (to use with thermometer)

Nylon, slip-lead leash

first aid **saline solution** Sterile Saline Eye Wash ANTIBACTERIAL

Sterile saline eye wash (to flush dirt or objects from the eye)

Tick removal tool (Don't use tweezers or a hot match!)

Rectal thermometer (to measure body temperature)

Pet nail clippers (to trim nails that are too long)

Restraint muzzle (Don't try to put this on an injured dog yourself; ask an adult.)

Bath towel (to wrap an injured dog)

PREVENT HOLIDAYS FROM TURNING INTO HOWLIDAYS

Throughout the year, your family will likely host picnics, celebrate holidays, and hold other special occasions that can generate lots of people (and even visiting pets) in your house. During these times, the normal household routine and decor get a major makeover that can spike your dog's curiosity or her stress level.

From your dog's perspective, shiny, dangling ornaments, tinsel, candles, and potpourri may be too hard to ignore. To keep special occasions as well as the holidays from turning into the "howlidays" with an emergency trip to the veterinary hospital, keep the following safety tips in mind.

WEAR HER OUT. Take her for a long walk or schedule mini play sessions of her favorite game, such as fetch or tug-of-war. Remember, a tired dog is a happy dog who is less likely to be looking for ways to get into trouble.

LET HER MINGLE. A people-loving, well-mannered dog can take the spotlight briefly to greet guests or perform a few tricks. Kona loves to sit up and extend a paw to say hello. But if your canine buddy begins to get overly excited, take her for a walk or give her some quiet time away from the action.

OR LET HER HIDE. Give a shy dog a safe place when the home is filled with guests. Usher her into a spare bedroom or other safe, closed room during the festivities. Provide her with a treat-filled toy or a chew bone to keep her busy.

WATCH THE DECORATIONS. For Halloween, Christmas, or other holidays involving decorations, go with battery-operated candles to avoid the risk of flames or hot wax that could harm your dog. Don't use breakable ornaments. They can cut your dog's paws — or worse, she could bite into them and cut her mouth.

WATCH THE FOOD. Holidays usually mean lots of special food to be kept out of paw's reach. Don't put gifts of food under a holiday tree where your dog can tear into them. If you have a dog who attempts to "counter surf" to steal goodies from kitchen counters or tables, confine her in a safe room when food is being served.

Common holiday food dangers for dogs are bread dough, sugary ham, and chocolate candies (see page 47 for other dangerous foods).

Answers to Trivia Quizzes

QUIZ 1 (PAGE 23)

1. **A.** People have the most taste buds, with about 9,000. Dogs have about 1,700 taste buds and cats have only 473. Veterinarians have discovered that dogs do not crave salty tastes like people do, but dogs do have special taste receptors to detect fat and water.

2. **D.** Greyhound. The long-legged, lightweight greyhound has a lot of spring in his legs. In fact, the world record canine leap was 5 feet, 8 inches high, achieved by a greyhound aptly named Soaring Cindy.

3. **C.** 12. With their excellent hearing, it's no surprise that dogs have about a dozen muscles to move their ears in various ways. They can rotate them to hear noises, perk them up to show interest, or flatten them when nervous or afraid.

4. **C.** Basenji. This hunting dog originated in central Africa. Known as the "barkless dog," the basenji is known for yodeling. (Surprise: Australian shepherds come from the American West!)

QUIZ 2 (PAGE 55)

1. **D.** When two dogs meet, the art of sniffing another dog's back end is known as the doggy handshake. Dogs are terrific sniffers. In fact, dogs can smell 10,000 times better than people can. And the rear end is where the anus and anal glands are located. They create secretions that give the sniffing dog clues about the sniffed dog's sex, social status in the pack, mood, and most recent meal. Pretty cool, right?

2. **B.** Dogs can see better than people in dim light, thanks to a special eye membrane called the tapetum lucidum. But they cannot see in total darkness. If you have an older dog at home, talk to your parents about plugging in a night light to help your dog navigate to the water bowl at night.

3. **C.** 1,700. Dogs, just like you, have taste buds to detect bitter, sweet, sour, and salty tastes. But you have about 9,000 taste buds! You can

taste foods far better than your dog. Dogs do have special taste receptors that enable them to taste fat and water, though.

4. **C.** 50 eggs in just one day. The most common areas for fleas to hide on a dog are the neck and on the back near the tail. Make sure your dog is on a flea and tick preventive medicine available at your veterinary clinic. This way, you can save your dog from flea bites and itches.

5. **A.** Dogs mostly cool off by panting, but they do have sweat glands in their paw pads. On a hot day, your dog might jump at the chance to dunk his "dogs" in a puddle from the hose!

QUIZ 3 (PAGE 90)

1. **D.** All of the above. It doesn't matter that you feed your dog healthy meals or keep him in stock with fun toys; he is demonstrating the mentality of his undomesticated ancestors who would bury surplus food in hiding spots to come back to later. It seems weird to us, but to your dog, dirt makes the treat taste better. And, finally dogs, who think "mine, mine, mine!" hide their treasures from other four-leggers so they don't have to share.

2. **C.** Dogs don't yawn when they are excited. But yawning isn't only a sign of being tired or bored. If your dog is yawning while there are loud sounds, he is telling you he is feeling anxious or nervous. Usher him away from those irritating sounds. If your dog yawns during training lessons, that's your cue to stop or introduce a new trick.

3. **A.** Grapes. It's fine to give your dog carrots, apple slices, or pieces of broiled chicken as rewards, but never toss your dog a grape. He could choke, and even scarier, too many grapes (or raisins) can be toxic for dogs.

4. **C.** Although researchers don't really know why dogs like to roll in disgusting things, many people think that dogs are covering up their own scent so they can sneak up on unsuspecting prey.

Another reason is that dogs don't like to smell like roses or lavender after a bath. Those strong artificial scents can irritate sensitive noses. Do your dog a favor and use unscented pet shampoo so he won't be tempted to dash into the backyard to roll in something that he thinks smells a whole lot better!

Resources

American Kennel Club
www.akc.org

American Society for the Prevention
of Cruelty to Animals
www.aspca.org

American Veterinary Medical
Association
www.avma.org

The Association of Pet Dog Trainers
www.apdt.com

Canine Learning Centers
www.k9lrng.com

Doggone Safe
www.doggonesafe.com

Dogster Magazine
www.dogster.com

Fear Free
www.fearfreepets.com

FetchFind
www.fetchfind.com

Fido Friendly Magazine
www.fidofriendly.com

The Humane Society of the
United States
www.humanesociety.org

Pet Life Radio
www.petliferadio.com

Pro Pet Hero
www.propethero.com

Preventive Vet
www.preventivevet.com

METRIC CONVERSIONS

Unless you have finely calibrated measuring equipment, conversions between US and metric measurements will be somewhat inexact. It's important to convert the measurements for all of the ingredients in a recipe to maintain the same proportions as the original. Here are a few common amounts used in recipes.

COOKING

US	METRIC
1 teaspoon	5 milliliters
1 tablespoon	15 milliliters
¼ cup	60 milliliters
½ cup	120 milliliters
1 cup	240 milliliters
2 cups	480 milliliters

LENGTH

TO CONVERT	TO	MULTIPLY
inches	centimeters	inches by 2.54
inches	meters	inches by 0.0254
feet	meters	feet by 0.3048
feet	kilometers	feet by 0.0003048

Recommended Reading

Canine Sports and Games by Kristin Mehus-Roe, Storey Publishing, 2009

Careers with Dogs by Kim Campbell Thornton, CompanionHouse Books, 2011

Chow Hounds by Ernie Ward, DVM, Health Communications, Inc., 2010

Lucky Dog Lessons: Train Your Dog in 7 Days by Brandon McMillan, HarperOne, 2016

Your Dog: The Owner's Manual by Marty Becker and Gina Spadafori, Grand Central Life & Style, 2011

OTHER BOOKS BY ARDEN MOORE

The Dog Behavior Answer Book, Storey Publishing, 2006

Fit Dog: Tips and Tricks to Give Your Pet a Longer, Healthier, Happier Life, Firefly Books, 2015

Real Food for Dogs, Storey Publishing, 2001

What Dogs Want: A Visual Guide to Understanding Your Dog's Every Move, Firefly Books, 2012

ACKNOWLEDGMENTS

I salute all the animal behaviorists, veterinarians, and professional dog trainers who have guided me for the past two decades of learning all things d-o-g. Special thanks go to Dr. Marty Becker, Dr. Alice Moon-Fanelli, Jamie Migdal, and Brandon McMillian.

This book would not be possible without dog-loving kids — our next generation of canine advocates. I love giving kids the tools they need to bring out the best in pets. I give special thanks to Terri Hooks and all the cool kids attending the SPCA of Texas critter camp for motivating me to write this book for kids everywhere.

Finally, I extend gratitude and appreciation to Lisa Hiley, my main editor, and the entire Storey Publishing team, who have believed in me since they published my first book nearly 20 years ago.

Index

Additional photography by © 2014 A Dogs Life Photography/stock.adobe.com, 76; © adogslifephoto/iStock.com, 38, 39, 69 b., 85 b.; © alexei_tm/iStock.com, 25 t.l., 31 b.; © aluxum/iStock.com, 42 (paint); © Andrey_Kuzmin/iStock.com, 129; © Anna_Rostova/iStock.com, 50; © annaav/stock.adobe.com, 118; © anntronova/stock.adobe.com, 27 t.; © Arden Moore, 6; © BillionPhotos.com/stock.adobe.com, 137; © chalabala/stock.adobe.com, 35; © ChristopherBernard/iStock.com, 40; © claireliz/stock.adobe.com, 30 b.; © damedeeso/iStock.com, 5, 132; © Eriklam/iStock.com, 24, 25 b.; © Ermolaev Alexandr/stock.adobe.com, 47 b., 131 b.; © exzozis/stock.adobe.com, 29 b.; © Fly_dragonfly/stock.adobe.com, 11 t.; © fotyma/iStock.com, 25 t.r.; © GeorgePeters/iStock.com, 59; © GlobalP/iStock.com, 11 b., 16, 95, 108 b., 127, 128 b.; © godrick/iStock.com, 117; © gollykim/iStock.com, 3, 31 t., 98; © GoodLifeStudio/iStock.com, 30 t.; © HadelProductions/iStock.com, 90 b.; © helga1981/stock.adobe.com, 122; © hhelene/stock.adobe.com, 41 (bittersweet); © igorr1/iStock.com, 28 b.; © IndigoLT/iStock.com, 104; © Javier brosch/stock.adobe.com, 52; © leungchopan/stock.adobe.com, 26 b.r.; © LIGHTFIELD STUDIOS/stock.adobe.com, 23, 55, 90 t.; © Liliboas/iStock.com, 15, 47 t., 53, 69 t., 79, 85 t., 128 t., 131 t.; © Marcelo-Kaneshira/iStock.com, 26 t.r.; © marcoventuriniautieri/iStock.com, 102; © MarkCoffeyPhoto/iStock.com, 94; © matka_Wariatka /iStock.com, 41 (tulip); © mato181/iStock.com, 31 m.; © Merril Buckhorn/iStock.com, 93; © mgstock /stock.adobe.com, 26 b.l.; © Michael Burrell/iStock.com, 41 (holly); © Mira Drozdowski/stock.adobe.com, 41 (rhododendron); © mwilson_93/iStock.com, 96; © nadisja/iStock.com, 126; © nataba/stock.adobe.com, 9; © nechaev-kon/iStock.com, 41 (buttercup); © Nerthuz/iStock.com, 44; © Nikolai Tsvetkov/stock.adobe.com, 65; © Orbon Alija/iStock.com, 101; © otsphoto /stock.adobe.com, 29 m., 97; © Parilov/stock.adobe.com, 46; © pauchi/stock.adobe.com, 115; © Pekic/iStock.com, 133; © PhotonStock/iStock.com, 42 (pillow); © rodimovpavel/stock.adobe.com, 73; © RyanJLane/iStock.com, 18; © Sam Edwards/Getty Images, 14; © scisettialfio/iStock.com, 41 (foxglove, oleander); © sdominick/iStock.com, 17; © SKapl/iStock.com, 130; © Soloviova Liudmyla/stock.adobe.com, 28 t.; © SolStock/iStock.com, 119; © SStajic/iStock.com, 29 t.; © svetography/stock.adobe.com, 21; © Tanaphong/iStock.com, 42 (tire); © Tara Gregg/EyeEm/Getty Images, 26 t.l.; © Tropical studio/stock.adobe.com, 30 m., 100; © ulkas/stock.adobe.com, 12; © unpict/iStock.com, 41 (yew); © Vasyl Dolmatov/stock.adobe.com, 136; © vikarus/iStock.com, 27 b.; © WilleeCole/iStock.com, 91; © Wojciech Kozielczyk/iStock.com, 51; © YinYang/iStock.com, 13

With thanks to the dogs whose star power shines so brightly in these pages:

- **BROOKS,** a springer spaniel who loves tug-of-war
- **CHANCE,** a Yorkshire terrier rescued from life as a breeder in a puppy mill
- **CHICO,** a miniature poodle and retired chief security officer
- **ODIN,** a rescued terrier mix who loves to snuggle under a heap of blankets
- **OTTO,** a senior citizen who brings daily cheer to someone even older than he is
- **PIPPIN,** a rescued puppy who loves his boy Nate
- **TESSA,** a patient Siberian husky with beautiful baby-blue eyes